Dark Shadow, Golden Shadow

Dark Shadow, Golden Shadow

MAGICKAL TOOLS AND TAROT
to confront your fears & free your potential

SHANNON KNIGHT

WEISER BOOKS

This edition first published in 2025 by Weiser Books, an imprint of
Red Wheel/Weiser, LLC
With offices at:
65 Parker Street, Suite 7
Newburyport, MA 01950
www.redwheelweiser.com

ISBN: 978-1-57863-892-5

Library of Congress Cataloging-in-Publication Data
Names: Knight, Shannon, 1989- author Title: Dark shadow, golden shadow : magickal tools and tarot
to confront your fears and free your potential / Shannon Knight.
Description: Newburyport, MA : Weiser Books, 2025. | Includes bibliographical references. |
Summary: " Unlike other books on the subject of shadow work, this one incorporates tarot as a prominent tool that serves as a method of self-reflection, offering a portal to our subconscious and helping
us access parts of ourselves that we otherwise may have been unable to. The imagery and archetypes
help facilitate a dialogue with our shadow, making it easier to converse with the repressed and hidden
parts of ourselves--both challenging (the dark) and positive (the golden)."-- Provided by publisher.
Identifiers: LCCN 2025023308 | ISBN 9781578638925 trade paperback | ISBN 9781633413863
ebook Subjects: LCSH: Tarot | Magic | BISAC: BODY, MIND & SPIRIT / Inspiration & Personal
Growth | BODY, MIND & SPIRIT / Healing / General Classification: LCC BF1879.T2 K587 2025
| DDC 131--dc23/eng/20250904
LC RECORD AVAILABLE AT HTTPS://LCCN.LOC.GOV/2025023308

Cover and interior by Sky Peck Design
Cover photograph © Getty Images
Tarot card images from *The Weiser Tarot* © Red Wheel/Weiser. All rights reserved
Typeset in Adobe Aldine

Printed in the United States of America
IBI

10 9 8 7 6 5 4 3 2 1

◆◆━◆◆

My ability to write on the topic of shadow work exists only because of the foundational work of the psychologists, psychotherapists, researchers, and analysts who have been pioneers in the field of psychology and the concept of the shadow. I am acutely aware that what I present here is not original, but rather a distillation of the vast and respected knowledge these thinkers have contributed to the field. It is a privilege to have the opportunity to explore and share even a fraction of their insights, along with my interpretations and experiences of such, with all of you. This work stands on the shoulders of those who have dedicated their lives to understanding the complexities of the human experience, and it is through their efforts that any meaningful exploration of these concepts is possible.

To every listener and follower of *The Tarot Diagnosis* podcast:
your support, interest, and curiosity have been empowering and
healing. Thank you for embracing my creativity and finding value in
the intersection of tarot and mental health.
This book is for you.

If we are able to see our own shadow and can bear knowing about it,
then a small part of the problem has already been solved:
we have at least brought up the personal unconscious.

—CARL JUNG

Contents

INTRODUCTION

For as long as tarot has existed in my world, I have favored the archetype of the Moon. As a young child and then eventually a teenager, I was always drawn to the dark and the mysterious. The idea of uncovering something hidden or undesirable to the rest of the world was alluring. Even now, I favor occult-themed trinkets, tarot cards, preserved insects, and animal bones I have plucked along secluded nature trails and remote hiking paths. The rush and excitement of discovering something not yet held, or that may otherwise have been forever hidden, buried under brush or washed away with the elements, are in many ways comforting. Holding space for and honoring these discoveries feel like paying homage to their existence.

It's no wonder I became a psychotherapist. Now I have the privilege of sitting across from folks every single day, bearing witness to the deepest, sometimes darkest depths of a human's soul. My work is rooted firmly within the archetype of the Moon, and by default, the shadow. My practice is dedicated to helping individuals navigate the terrain of their internal and external worlds, promoting self-reflection, compassion, curiosity, growth, and healing. By integrating a variety of tools beyond traditional modalities, such as tarot, I find profound insights and deeper self-awareness emerge, especially as we travel through the often daunting world of the shadow.

Much like my affinity for the archetype of the Moon, my fascination with the shadow has persisted from the moment I learned of its existence. It was my first year of undergraduate school, and I was the only freshman in an Analytical Psychology class full of juniors and seniors. The room was small and narrow with noisy floorboards. I remember admiring the detailed molding around the drafty windows and wondering what types of people had peered through its glass. The noisy floorboards along with the Moorish minarets, architectural domes, and cupolas were not the only remnants of its rich history, though. The building was originally a hotel built in the late 1800s. Before all the moving around and college transferring I did, I attended the University of Tampa. Plant Hall, the building where my psychology classes were held, hosted the likes of Teddy Roosevelt, the Queen of England, Stephen Crane, and Babe Ruth.

Each week I would walk into class and feel the energy of the last 120 years that had embedded itself into the walls of the university. It always felt magickal. The historic energy was amplified by one of my professors, an older gentleman with silver hair and a thick, white mustache. He looked like a stockier version of Sam Elliott. I wish I remembered his name. He had us reading the works of Sigmund Freud, Carl Jung, Karen Horney, and Rollo May—often transporting us back 100 years to discuss their theories and then formulate our own. This is when I first began to explore the concept of the shadow.

We spent a significant amount of time in that class parsing through Freud's book *The Ego and the Id*, which confused me beyond measure as an eighteen-year-old desperate to understand the human psyche. It was not until a few years later when I was in graduate school and I had several more psychology courses under my belt and a deeper understanding of Carl Jung's work that Freud's theories on the unconscious started to make sense to me. Eventually, I realized that Freud's theories of the unconscious mind, highlighted by what he called the "id," were driven purely by primal urges and instincts. On the other hand, Jung's theories on the unconscious mind highlighted the parts of ourselves that we have rejected, repressed, or my favorite, not yet discovered. This is what Jung called the shadow and what would eventually become the focal point of what we refer to today as shadow work.

During my studies, I learned that many occult communities had claimed the works of Carl Jung as a foundation of their practices. This revelation was intriguing as a psychology nerd who was dabbling in the world of the occult. As a teenager, I would spend my afternoons studying and doing homework on the patio of my local metaphysical shop. The owners were clever and included a small bistro as part of their storefront. So after school I would grab a smoothie and sit in their courtyard to study. Shaded by a canopy of oak trees and perfumed by the bay just across the street, the salty air mixed with knowledge tucked away in the books I was reading felt like a comforting hug.

Looking back, I find humor and irony in that I began studying psychology as a sixteen-year-old, in the courtyard of a metaphysical store. A few decades later I finally figured out how to merge my two favorite schools of thought, through the work of *The Tarot Diagnosis* podcast and community. My hope is that within these pages you also find value in the merger of two different, but complementary worlds: shadow work and tarot. In your shadow work quest, I hope this book becomes your companion in helping you discover deeper layers of insight, self-compassion, and a more confident understanding of yourself. The work ahead may be challenging, but it's also profoundly rewarding.

HOW TO USE THIS BOOK

Given the vast and delicate nature of the shadow, it's impossible to cover every aspect of the shadow, the research around it, and the expansive rhetoric on the topic within the confines of this book. Instead, this book serves as an introductory guide to help you begin (or deepen) your shadow work journey. Each chapter offers insights, practical exercises, and reflective prompts designed to help you explore different facets of your shadow self.

As you engage with the material, keep in mind that shadow work is a very personal experience and a journey that is unique to everyone. Take your time with each exercise, reflect on your experiences, and be patient with yourself. Don't engage in this work if you are feeling emotionally fragile, anxious, or do not have adequate support or resources in place. It's best to have a supportive friend, therapist, coach, community, or confidant to lean on for support and empathy as you work through this material.

The Importance of Journaling

As an adjunct to this guidebook, I recommend keeping a journal because a lot will come up for you as you're both reviewing the material and completing the exercises. You'll want to keep a record of your thoughts, feelings, and experience. The many exercises throughout this book provide some space for your written responses but not enough to honor and record the depths of your insights that you'll undoubtedly reach. The sample journal pages throughout this book are titled "Reflect," and are meant to function as prompts and samples to encourage deeper reflective responses that you will want to record in your journal. In addition to providing a safe space for you to record the exercises in this book, your journal will no doubt contain all of the discoveries you make along your journey: You'll be able to track what triggers you, observe your emotional patterns and responses over time, and identify which exercises benefit you most. You'll discover your wounded parts as well as your "golden" parts—the talent and potential you didn't know you possessed, or perhaps were afraid to express. There is no right or wrong way to journal your experience throughout your shadow work journey. What matters is that you're committing to reflect in whatever way works best for you.

Dark Shadow, Golden Shadow has been designed for individuals who crave depth, creativity, and mysticism in their self-exploration journey. If you enjoy combining nontraditional healing methods, such as tarot, with evidenced-based practices in psychology, then you have come to the right place. Throughout this book, we will explore the complex depths of the conscious and unconscious mind, the value of the shadow, and the therapeutic and magickal methods of engaging in the process of shadow work.

During this journey, you will have the opportunity in each chapter to engage in a plethora of exercises dedicated to the shadow. The last chapter in this book is meant to function as a supplement to the previous chapters as it includes additional exercises that expand upon the concepts within this book.

Note: Many of these exercises involve the use of tarot as a tool to help you access deeper parts of yourself (like the unconscious) through archetypal symbols and imagery. However, the exercises can be done with other tools such as oracle cards (which also rely heavily on symbolism), or simply through personal reflection and journaling. What matters is that you choose a tool that you enjoy, feel connected to, and resonates with your practice.

THE BENEFITS OF SHADOW WORK

Shadow work is the process of acknowledging the repressed and rejected parts of ourselves and bringing those parts into our conscious awareness to help us feel whole, integrated, and self-aware. It might seem odd that exploring the parts of our identities that we deem unfavorable would have benefits, but without identifying and acknowledging these parts we deny ourselves true growth. This process ultimately leads to an increase in feelings of empowerment and self-compassion, as well as a deeper understanding of the human experience.

Shadow work also helps us to discover the root of some of our unhealthy and maladaptive behaviors and thought patterns. Once these patterns are identified, we are more likely to notice them in the future and then feel better prepared to modify them so that we can live authentically, intentionally, and with more internal and external peace.

It is also quite common to explore the concept of the shadow inside the therapy room. Clinicians are trained to safely bring clients into a state of self-awareness, helping clients navigate their internal container of shadows. As a therapist, I often help clients identify shadows through a series of carefully crafted questions based on my observations of their behavior and personal narratives. The foundation of the exercises throughout this book has been built upon these types of therapeutic interactions.

When we step into the container of our shadow, we unearth a wealth of insights about our deepest fears, desires, and motivations. This journey into the shadow is not just about addressing what we feel is "wrong" with us; it's about embracing the full spectrum of our humanity, acknowledging that every facet of our being has a place in our story. This type of radical acceptance fosters a more compassionate relationship with ourselves and, by extension, with others. It allows us to see the shared struggles and vulnerabilities that bind us all, creating a deep sense of interconnectedness and empathy.

Shadow work, especially in therapy, can also shed light on the dynamics of our platonic, romantic, and professional relationships. By recognizing how our shadows influence our interactions, we can begin to break cycles and unlearn patterns that perpetuate conflict or misunderstanding. This awareness paves the way for healthier, more authentic connections, where we feel seen and accepted for who we truly are. This process also allows us to hold space for, empathize with, and access greater patience when confronting the shadows of others. In essence, integrating shadow work into the therapeutic practice not only enriches our individual lives but also enhances our capacity to build deeper, more meaningful relationships with those around us.

ETHICAL CONSIDERATIONS

It's important for me as a therapist to start off each therapeutic relationship by making three very important statements. The first is, "I believe you are *the* expert on yourself. If I ever say anything that you feel does not accurately represent you, your feelings, or your experience, it's vital that you point that out to me." The second statement is, "This work, while beneficial and ultimately freeing, is often overwhelming and exhausting." The third statement is, "It sometimes gets worse before it gets better."

While this book is not a form of mental health counseling, these three statements still hold true when folks are navigating shadow work on their own or with someone they trust as a source of support. Ultimately, you are the expert on yourself. So if you are engaged in the practice of tarot, for example, and the cards are showing you something that just does not feel accurate or representative of you and your experience, then maybe it's not. There is no need to try to find meaning in something that you feel doesn't have meaning for you. Now, that does not mean you should avoid challenging yourself, because shadow work is inherently an act of challenging the Self.

Take this book, for example. The words I write are reflective of my own interpretations and experiences of psychology, shadow work, tarot, and the concept of magick. Some of this content you may resonate with deeply, some of it you will not. So, as folks in the magickal world might say, "Take what resonates and leave what doesn't."

Additionally, this work is not meant to be easy. Shadow work isn't a simple act or process. This is a commitment to be curious about your beliefs and personal narratives, which will ultimately lead to a change in the way you think and engage with your thoughts, feelings, and internal and external world. Being aware of your personal limits is vital as you embark on this journey. You might need to take breaks frequently. Perhaps you only engage in this work a few weeks out of the year, or maybe you reflect every day. Neither level of engagement is better or "healthier" than the other. It merely depends on your personal capacity for self-reflection along with the types of shadows you are exploring.

Facing our shadow parts means being willing to confront uncomfortable truths and challenge long-held beliefs about ourselves and others. This practice involves holding space for painful memories, recognizing harmful behaviors, and accepting parts of ourselves that might contradict the image we have worked hard to portray to the world. While some shadows might be easier to engage with, others may feel overwhelming. This is important personal data. The shadows that feel overwhelming may not be ready to be explored yet, so try not to force yourself to explore something that you are not entirely ready for. Additionally, some shadows are rooted in trauma, and if you have not yet processed this trauma with a professional, shadow work may not be appropriate at this time.

SETTING INTENTIONS FOR YOUR JOURNEY

Before beginning your shadow work journey, it's important to set clear intentions for yourself. Setting intentions helps to create a focused and meaningful path, and it grounds your efforts in a sense of purpose and clarity. Consider what you hope to achieve, the aspects of yourself you wish to understand better, and the insights you hope to uncover and integrate as you work your way through this material.

EXERCISE: IDENTIFYING INTENTIONS

Take a few moments to reflect on your reasons for engaging in shadow work.

- What areas of yourself do you wish to improve or understand better?

- What is the reason you want to engage in this work?

- What value does shadow work hold for you?

- What resistance to this work do you have?

Chapter 1

Exploring and Preparing for Shadow Work

❧

You can choose courage, or you can choose comfort,
but you cannot choose both.

—BRENÉ BROWN

WHAT IS SHADOW WORK?

Shadow work is the process of exploring and integrating the parts of ourselves that we have repressed, rejected, deemed unacceptable, or believe to be incompatible with our conscious self-image due to messaging we have received from others. This process demands deep and personal exploration that can sometimes be uncomfortable. However, despite the discomfort, by acknowledging and integrating our shadow, we inevitably reduce the power it can often have over us, which then creates space for us to access deeper layers of ourselves.

There are many parallels between shadow work and the therapeutic process. Both help clients uncover the root cause of their maladaptive behaviors, negative thought patterns, and emotional distress. In therapy, clients gradually wade into their subconscious, unearthing parts of themselves they have felt shame or fear around, and then learn how to manage and coexist with those parts. This is a process that occurs over months, and sometimes years. Even after therapy ends, the work continues as clients apply the insights gained in session to their everyday lives. Shadow work is no different; it's an ongoing journey that requires dedication, patience, and intention.

One of the most powerful aspects of shadow work is its ability to help us discover our "golden shadow," which contains the positive qualities and potential that we may have also repressed. The golden shadow can include untapped or suppressed potential related to creativity, intuition, and curiosity, among other qualities. By discovering and then embracing these golden shadows, we can enhance our lives and relationships, bringing our life a greater sense of purpose and fulfillment. Shadow work is not just about confronting the dark; it's also about reclaiming the full spectrum of who we are.

Essentially, the goal of shadow work is to move beyond the binary thought process of "good" and "bad" parts and instead step into a more nuanced understanding of ourselves and the world around us. To engage in shadow work requires a commitment to self-discovery, a healthy dose of self-compassion, and a large reservoir of curiosity. In the end, the rewards of insight, authenticity, and contentment are well worth the effort.

WHAT SHADOW WORK IS NOT

Shadow work is not about healing in the conventional sense or about eliminating the parts of ourselves that we dislike or that have been deemed "bad." It's also not a process that can be completed by reading a single book, attending a single workshop, writing in a single journal, or practicing a single meditation. Shadow work is a lifelong process that requires ongoing commitment and introspection. It's about recognizing and integrating the parts of ourselves that we have pushed away or hidden, not about eradicating them. The goal is not to "fix" ourselves, but to better understand and widen our capacity to be compassionate, insightful, and self-aware.

Often, shadow work is misunderstood as a process of discovering and then eliminating. However, consider the experience of intrusive thoughts: the more we try to push them away or get rid of them, the more persistent and demanding they become. When we invite these thoughts to take the stage for a moment (acknowledging their presence), they tend to loosen their grip on us. These thoughts may not disappear completely, but they are likely to become less invasive over time. Shadow work operates from a similar framework. By inviting our shadows to the forefront for a moment, we can decrease the unconscious power they may have over us. This process isn't about silencing or banishing these parts of ourselves, but about understanding their origins and the roles they play in our lives and how they impact our relationships, actions, and thought processes.

By recognizing our shadows, we allow them to exist without them feeling the need to dominate our lives. This form of radical acceptance is crucial for growth. However, it's not about transforming into an idealized version of ourselves. Instead, this journey is about acknowledging and becoming aware of our imperfections and complexities. In this way, shadow work teaches us that "healing" isn't about becoming whole by removing parts of ourselves, but about becoming whole by accepting all parts of ourselves. Remember, shadow work isn't a quick fix or a linear process.

PREPARING FOR SHADOW WORK

Beginning a shadow work journey is equal parts enlightening and daunting, and because of that, it's essential to have a solid foundation of coping skills and nervous system regulation techniques ready to go in your "emotional toolbox" before you begin to step into the depths of the shadow. As a gentle reminder, shadow work is not something that is completed in a day, a week, or a month. Shadow work is a commitment to looking inward, getting curious, and embracing vulnerability to explore aspects of the Self that have influenced our feelings and behaviors for years and sometimes even decades. Think about how long some of these shadow parts have been repressed; sometimes it can take just as long to process their existence and feel comfortable, safe, and prepared enough to invite them into conscious awareness.

Preparing for shadow work means learning how to self-regulate, a process that evolves with us as we age. Our childhood serves as the foundation upon which we build our emotional regulation abilities. The lessons we absorb during those formative years significantly influence how we respond to and manage our feelings throughout our lives. One fundamental concept at play here is learned behavior. Children are like sponges, absorbing information from their environment and the people around them constantly, especially their parents or caregivers.

When children grow up in an environment where they witness healthy emotional regulation, they're more likely to develop similar skills. They observe how their caregivers cope with stress, express their emotions, and handle conflicts in a way that makes them feel better and prioritizes the safety and well-being of those around them. These observations become the building blocks for their own emotional regulation toolbox. On the other hand, if a child is raised in an environment where emotional turmoil, outbursts, or emotional suppression are the norm, they may adopt these same behaviors as their own coping mechanisms because that is what they learned to do.

When individuals work on improving their emotional regulation skills, not only does this benefit themselves, it also creates a ripple effect within their families and relationships. As they break free from the unhealthy patterns learned in childhood, they become better equipped to model healthy emotional regulation for their own children and loved ones. This, in turn, helps prevent the perpetuation of unhealthy emotional patterns across generations and essentially breaks a cycle.

Take a moment to reflect on how you saw emotional regulation growing up.

- How did what you learned in childhood inform how you regulate your emotions as an adult?

Now think about coping skills or techniques you may have learned on your own that you have found to be helpful when you need to calm yourself down when you feel anxious, nervous, or on edge. It's okay if you haven't found anything that works for you yet. You will be invited to experiment by practicing different techniques and preparing your "emotional toolbox" for your shadow work journey in the next section.

- What are your current "go to" coping mechanisms?

CREATING A COPING SKILLS "TOOLBOX"

Shadow work is useless, and even detrimental, if we don't take time to regulate our nervous system. Shadow work involves confronting deeply buried emotions, unresolved trauma, and uncomfortable, repressed aspects of our Self. These encounters can trigger the body's stress response, leading to heightened anxiety, overwhelm, dissociation, or other uncomfortable responses. Knowing how to self-soothe, or regulate the nervous system, is vital to this process.

It's also important to know *when* you need to regulate. Pay attention to how you are feeling while you are self-reflecting and working your way through this book. You will know that it's time to regulate your nervous system if your heart starts beating faster, you become sweaty, irritable, or frustrated.

Regulating the nervous system ensures that we can approach shadow work with a grounded and balanced state of mind. It allows us to process intense emotions without being overwhelmed by them, facilitating a safer and more productive exploration of our inner world and various parts.

Because shadow work involves facing aspects of ourselves that we may have rejected, denied, or deemed unworthy, the process can stir up feelings of shame, guilt, and self-criticism. Knowing how to infuse self-compassion into this process is vital because it establishes a supportive and nonjudgmental environment for self-exploration. Self-compassion allows us to approach our shadow with curiosity and kindness rather than harsh judgment and criticism and creates a safe space for uncovering and then integrating the hidden parts of our psyche. This ultimately leads to feelings of balance and contentment.

Because shadow work often brings up difficult memories, emotions, and insights, it may challenge our existing beliefs and identity. This can be emotionally intense and at times draining. Preventing overwhelm ensures that we can engage in shadow work at a pace that suits our emotional readiness. It minimizes the risk of re-traumatization and allows us to maintain a sense of autonomy and control over our healing journey.

Sometimes we can only handle small doses of shadow work at a time, and that is okay. Find a pace that feels safe and sustainable for you. You may have to check in with yourself more often than you think to see if the pace you are working at needs to be modified or adjusted.

Shadow work should not be something you embark on if you do not feel adequately resourced. This means if you don't feel like you have the ability to handle facing difficult truths about yourself, because you may be struggling with stress, anxiety, or trauma that has not yet been addressed, then you may want to make shadow work a priority for a different time. Beyond that, if you are having a bad day or are feeling more self-critical than normal, these are cues that it might not be the best time to step into the world of the shadow.

Now, you don't have to be perfectly "healed" or have all the stars aligned to do this work—that is impossible. However, it's important that you feel like you are in the space where you can receive and explore potentially difficult information about yourself and approach it with compassion and curiosity.

EMOTIONAL REGULATION TECHNIQUES

Below are a few common techniques for emotional regulation you may want to utilize throughout your shadow work journey. In the spaces provided, take some time to reflect on how you experienced each exercise after practicing it. Use the scales to note how easy or helpful each technique felt. Remember, these exercises are meant to help steady the stress responses that might flare up as we dive into shadow work. They are here to remind us that we are more than just our shadows. Sometimes, though, our minds fixate on a single aspect of ourselves, which can stir up discomfort. This is when it's crucial to pause, practice the emotional regulation techniques, and bring ourselves back into a more balanced and grounded state.

Diaphragmatic Breathing

Diaphragmatic breathing, also known as belly breathing, is probably the most popular and arguably the most powerful technique for reducing stress and promoting relaxation. It helps lower cortisol levels (the body's primary stress hormone) and activates the parasympathetic nervous system, which regulates the body's rest-and-digest response. This practice, when combined with humming, also stimulates the vagus nerve, which plays a key role in controlling the nervous system and maintaining balance.

Belly breathing is an often-overlooked tool for calming the nervous system because many folks don't realize the depth of benefits that simply focusing on something we each do automatically every second of the day can have. Yet the research is astounding. In fact, a 2019 study called "Effectiveness of Diaphragmatic Breathing for Reducing Physiological and Psychological Stress in Adults" showed that just one session of twenty minutes of diaphragmatic breathing yielded beneficial health results. This same study found that belly breathing led to a decrease in blood pressure, cortisol (the stress hormone), and overall stress markers.

INSTRUCTIONS

Sit or lie down in a comfortable position. Ensure your back is straight if you are sitting, and if lying down, keep your legs slightly bent with feet flat on the floor or extended comfortably.

Close your eyes and take a moment to relax your body. Release any tension in your shoulders, jaw, and neck by imagining the tension melting into the chair or floor. Work your way down through each muscle group in your body, imagining each muscle slowly releasing tension and becoming flexible and less rigid.

Place one hand on your chest and the other on your abdomen, just below your rib cage. This will help you feel the movement of your diaphragm as you breathe.

Take a slow, deep breath in through your nose, allowing your abdomen to rise as you fill your lungs with air. Imagine your belly is a balloon and by breathing in you are filling the balloon with air and watching it expand. Your chest should remain relatively still while your belly expands. Count to four as you inhale.

Hold your breath for a moment (about two seconds).

Exhale slowly through your mouth, allowing your abdomen to fall as you release the air. Count to four as you exhale. Focus on emptying your lungs completely. If you would like to add an additional relaxation method to stimulate the vagus nerve, you can hum during your exhale. This technique allows the vibration of the hum to have a soothing effect on your nervous system.

Continue this breathing pattern for a few cycles, focusing on the rise and fall of your abdomen with each breath. When your mind wanders (because it will and that is completely normal), gently bring your attention back to your breath.

⇒ *Reflect* ⇐

How did your body respond to the diaphragmatic breathing exercise?

_____

_____

Did you notice any changes in muscle tension or physical sensations?

_____

_____

What type of resistance did you notice, if any?

_____

_____

How could you integrate diaphragmatic breathing into your shadow work journey to help regulate your emotions and manage discomfort?

_____

_____

EASE OF USE

How easy was it for you to perform this exercise?
(1 = Very Difficult, 5 = Very Easy)

1   2   3   4   5

HELPFULNESS

How helpful was this exercise in regulating stress or calming your mind?
(1 = Not Helpful, 5 = Extremely Helpful)

1   2   3   4   5

IDENTIFYING INNATE VALUE

Another integral component in our coping skills toolbox is being able to identify our innate value. Shadow work involves looking at the parts of us that we try to ignore, forget, or hide away. These are the parts of us that often increase feelings of insecurity, low self-esteem, or low self-worth. However, duality is present within each of us. Even though we all have shadow parts, we also have golden shadows. For example, we might have moments of intense jealousy or envy but also be encouraging and supportive. Holding space for opposing traits and qualities allows us to feel internally balanced. As humans, we are complex and that is okay.

This exercise encourages the exploration of our inherent value with the goal of increasing self-compassion and self-esteem.

Take a moment to reflect on some of your positive qualities, talents, and strengths and begin making a list of them. These can be any skills, personality traits, or accomplishments no matter how insignificant you might think they are. Write down at least two positive qualities that you genuinely appreciate about yourself.

For example: "I am compassionate," "I am a good listener," "I am creative," etc.

If this is difficult, think about compliments you have received from others.

1. _____

2. _____

Now think about past accomplishments and successes in your life, no matter how big or small. These can be academic, personal, or professional achievements.

Write down a few of these achievements and reflect on the skills and determination that helped you reach them.

1. _____

2. _____

Consider instances where you have shown kindness or made a positive impact on someone else's life. These can be simple acts of kindness or more significant gestures.

Write down at least three instances where you have been kind or made a difference in someone's life.

1. _____

2. _____

3. _____

Self-discovery and building self-confidence and self-compassion are ongoing processes. By consistently practicing these exercises and nurturing your self-worth, you can enhance your overall well-being and approach not only shadow work, but also life's challenges with greater resilience and confidence.

⇒ *Reflect* ⇐

When you reflect on your positive qualities and strengths, how do you feel about acknowledging them?

_____

_____

_____

_____

_____

Is there any discomfort or resistance that arises?

_____

_____

_____

_____

_____

EASE OF USE

How easy was it for you to perform this exercise?
(1 = Very Difficult, 5 = Very Easy)

1   2   3   4   5

HELPFULNESS

How helpful was this exercise in regulating your stress or calming your mind?
(1 = Not Helpful, 5 = Extremely Helpful)

1   2   3   4   5

CREATING A SAFE AND SACRED SPACE

The space in which we engage in any sort of personal, healing, or magickal journey can have a significant impact on how we feel and engage in that experience. Are you someone who needs a completely quiet place when you are pulling tarot cards, journaling, or reading? Maybe you are someone who must have background noise or music playing while you are working. Perhaps clutter makes it impossible for you to focus. Think about how you engage with your personal space or your environment.

I tend to feel moments of profound healing when I am out in nature. So my best, most productive and self-reflective work tends to happen when I am outside on the patio, in the garden, hiking, sitting beside a body of water, or resting in a hammock under the stars at night. What is interesting about knowing this part of me is that usually that means I don't have, or even need, a lot of tools accessible to engage in healing, shadow, or magickal work. I simply just need myself and nature. However, this isn't the case for everyone. For example, I work with many folks in my therapy practice who have to have a notebook with them each session, along with something to fidget with, and maybe even a beverage (or two) because these tools help them stay focused, remain engaged, and feel safe. We will be exploring a variety of tools and aids that might be helpful to you in this process in a later chapter.

Something to keep in mind is that shadow work can happen anywhere, anytime. For example, once you become aware of your shadow you might notice it when interacting with friends, in the middle of a work meeting, while grocery shopping, etc. When you feel like you are able to regulate your nervous system and have the capacity to engage with your shadow in these spaces, shadow work could mean you take a moment to notice the experience, and then later remember to ask yourself a few questions about what came up for you in that moment and what that may say about you, once you are in a space that feels safe to explore this.

One of the most important aspects of shadow work that often gets overlooked is figuring out what you need to feel safe, grounded, and open. Everyone's needs look different, and taking the time to understand what helps you feel secure and present can make all the difference in this work.

This is not just about comfort, it's also about emotional regulation. When we feel safe, our nervous system settles, and we are better able to access the deeper parts of ourselves that may be hidden, like the shadow.

For some folks, that might mean building a ritual around their practice, such as lighting a candle, burning incense, or laying out a few crystals that feel meaningful to them. These small acts can serve as gentle cues to your body and brain that it's time to go inward for some focused work. We will dig deeper into ritual and tools in another chapter, but for now, just know that you have permission to experiment. Try different combinations and notice what feels most supportive. Maybe it's the earthy smell of patchouli, the flicker and warmth of candlelight, or the cool weight of a particular stone in your hand. Whatever it is, let it comfort and ground you in this work.

Never underestimate the power of sensory input, either. The space you are in matters and can make a huge difference in this journey. You want it to feel like an invitation, not a confrontation since this work is inherently confrontational. Think soft textures, cozy nooks, and lighting that doesn't send your nervous system into overdrive (seriously—if you're anything like me, fluorescent lighting is the *enemy*). Sound is also important. Silence can be unsettling for some people, so maybe you play ambient nature sounds, white or brown noise, or something soft and instrumental in the background. The more your environment supports your sensory and nervous system needs, the more likely you are to feel safe enough to do the deep, meaningful work that shadow exploration requires.

Finally, integrating mindfulness practices into your routine can help you stay grounded and present during shadow work. Simple techniques like the deep breathing we explored earlier, meditation, or mindful movement can prepare your mind and body for the introspective journey. Before diving into shadow work, always take a few moments to center yourself. If you have been running around all day, immediately sitting down to work with the shadow is not recommended. Instead, create an intentional moment and close your eyes, take a few deep breaths, and allow yourself to settle. You are always invited to revisit the belly breathing exercise at the beginning of this chapter anytime you need to. This mindful approach not only calms the nervous system but also heightens your awareness, making it easier to recognize and process the emotions and thoughts that arise during shadow work. By incorporating these practices, you create a stable foundation from which to explore the depths of your shadow.

CREATING A SHADOW WORK ALTAR

While many people associate altars with religion, witchcraft, or spirituality, they have a broader history and purpose. In fact, we often create informal altars in our everyday lives without realizing it. For example, think about your kitchen setup around the coffee maker or tea kettle, with mugs, sugar, and other items within reach; this is essentially an altar, a thoughtfully arranged space that serves a particular purpose. Altars can function as secular spaces that invite groundedness and intentionality.

A workspace altar might include items that stimulate creativity and productivity: a favorite pen, a notebook, a small plant, or a photo. This setup transforms a mundane desk into a space where work becomes a mindful practice imbued with personalization and intention. Altars can also evolve with us over time, reflecting our changing needs and desires. Seasonal decorating, for example, could be seen as an altar space, like decorating a fireplace mantel.

Creating and maintaining an altar can also be a grounding ritual in and of itself. The process of arranging and tending to your altar is similar to a psychodrama exercise in psychotherapy and invites creativity and mindfulness. In this way, altars become more than just physical spaces; they are dynamic, lively practices that nurture our spirit and enhance our daily lives.

EXERCISE: BUILDING AN ALTAR

The act of creating an altar can be an act of self-compassion. We know that engaging in shadow work can be draining and stir up difficult emotions. So, think about items that bring you comfort that you might want to keep at your shadow work altar. For example, nature is vital to my well-being, which means I always keep plants on my desk or altar. Plants or fresh flowers make me feel connected to the earth, help me feel grounded, and are relaxing to look at while I am reflecting, pulling cards, or journaling. Examples of items you might want to include in your shadow work altar could be: plants, stones, incense, photos, a journal, a tarot deck, jewelry or a statue representing something important to you, artwork, books, lotion, essential oil, etc. I try to incorporate something that tends to all of my senses.

Since altar spaces are unique to everyone, there is no "right way" to create or set up an altar—especially when you are creating one for personal reflection or shadow work. As you prepare to create your own altar, you might find there are suggestions and guidelines for altars based on different religious or spiritual practices. If your beliefs align with one of those practices, then it might be comforting to set up your shadow work altar to align with those suggestions and guidelines. The important part is that your altar feels safe and soothing.

⇒ *Reflect* ⇐

What specific items or symbols make you feel grounded and safe, and how can you incorporate these into your shadow work altar to support your emotional well-being?

_____

_____

_____

_____

What specific intention do you want your shadow work altar to embody, and how can you arrange your items to reflect that purpose?

_____

_____

_____

_____

How will you maintain or evolve your altar as you progress through your shadow work, ensuring it continues to meet your emotional needs?

_____

_____

_____

_____

ASSESSING YOUR READINESS
FOR SHADOW WORK

While preparing for shadow work is a vital first step on this journey, understanding when to start, stop, or pause shadow work is also crucial for your emotional well-being and personal growth. Choosing to explore the parts of ourselves that we have denied, hidden, and repressed is not an easy feat. Because the shadow often contains trauma, pain, and truths that can feel confusing and uncomfortable, we need to prioritize assessing our readiness for this work.

The questions below will help you gauge your readiness for shadow work and help you recognize the signs that indicate whether you should continue, if you should take a brief break, or if you should pause your shadow work journey for an extended period.

Readiness Questionnaire

Take a moment to reflect on the following questions.

- Emotional Readiness

  How do I feel when I think about confronting my shadow parts?

  Am I experiencing any strong emotions such as fear, anxiety, or overwhelm?

  Do I feel emotionally stable and supported in my current environment?

- Physical and Mental Well-being

  How is my physical health? Am I getting enough rest and caring for my body?

  Do I have any mental health concerns that need immediate attention before diving into shadow work?

- Support System

  Do I have a reliable support system, such as friends, family, or a therapist, to lean on during this process?

Am I able to openly communicate my needs and boundaries with my support system?

- Time and Commitment

  Do I have the time to dedicate to regular self-reflection and shadow work exercises?

  Am I prepared to commit to this process, knowing it can be long-term and ongoing?

Recognizing When to Pause or Stop Shadow Work

It is essential to recognize when you need to take a break or pause your shadow work. Use the reflection questions below to gauge how you are feeling during your shadow work journey. Revisit this assessment regularly.

- Identifying Overwhelm

  Am I feeling constantly overwhelmed or anxious during or after shadow work sessions?

  Do I find it difficult to cope with daily life due to the emotional toll of shadow work?

- Physical and Mental Health Check

  Have I noticed any decline in my physical or mental health since starting shadow work?

  Am I neglecting self-care or other responsibilities because of the intensity of the work?

- Evaluating Support and Safety

  Do I feel unsupported or unsafe while exploring my shadow parts?

  Am I able to discuss my feelings and experiences with my support system without fear of judgment?

Window of Tolerance

The "window of tolerance" is a concept introduced by Dr. Dan Siegel, to describe the ideal range of emotional arousal where a person can function effectively in daily life. We have a comfort zone, a stretch zone, and a panic zone. The comfort zone is where we function optimally and feel safe and at ease. The stretch zone is where we begin to feel challenged but are still within a range of emotion that is manageable. The panic zone is where we feel acutely uncomfortable, overwhelmed, and reactive. This panic zone is where shadow work, if not approached carefully, may push us too far, triggering fight, flight, or freeze responses.

Noticing when we are approaching the edge of our comfort zone and entering the stretch zone allows us to work within our limits, pacing our growth rather than plunging into emotional overload. This model reinforces the importance of self-compassion and patience as we engage with the shadow.

EXERCISE: WINDOW OF TOLERANCE

Use the tarot spread below to help identify your personal window of tolerance by pulling cards to represent your comfort, stretch, and panic zones. Reflect on how this insight can help you assess your emotional states as you progress through your shadow work journey.

Card 1: Comfort. When do I feel most at home, comfortable, and safe?

Card 2: Stretch. How do I know when my boundaries and comfort levels are being tested?

Card 3: Panic. How do I know when I have passed my limits?

Reflect

My cards for this exercise are:

Card 1: _____

Thoughts: _____

_____

_____

_____

Card 2: _____

Thoughts: _____

_____

_____

_____

Card 3: _____

Thoughts: _____

_____

_____

_____

Chapter 2

Roots of the Shadow

There is, in fact, no access to the unconscious and to our own reality but through the shadow.

—CONNIE ZWEIG

DEFINING THE SHADOW

The concept of shadow work is rooted in the work and theories of Carl Gustav Jung, a Swiss psychiatrist and founder of analytical psychology. In his book, *The Psychology of the Unconscious*, Jung theorized that the concept of the shadow contained traits, thoughts, and beliefs we hold about ourselves that we want to avoid acknowledging. While Jung coined the term and concept of the shadow, he did not directly talk about "shadow work" but instead used terms like "shadow integration and assimilation."

Essentially, Jung believed that our shadow represents the parts of our identity that we consciously or unconsciously distance ourselves from because we perceive these parts to be negative or undesirable. However, the shadow is not just about "good" versus "bad" parts and instead functions within an entire internal system that requires us to work with it, instead of against it.

Throughout this book, the term *shadow* refers to the parts of ourselves that we suppress, deny, or repress—often shaped by societal expectations, cultural norms, childhood experiences, guilt, shame, or trauma. These shadow parts represent the aspects of ourselves we have learned to keep hidden so we could safely develop into the person or identity we believed was expected of us by caregivers or others whose love and approval we sought. Our shadows are frequently born out of the real or perceived rejection we have experienced and become activated when parts of us feel misaligned with who we believe we *should* be or who we think others want or need us to be.

While these suppressed parts of our Self can include our fears, insecurities, unacknowledged desires, unresolved conflicts, and traits and characteristics that others may have deemed "undesirable," the shadow can also include our special interests, sexuality, and creativity. Not only does our shadow encompass traits about ourselves we dislike, but it often leads us to dislike these same traits in others. In fact, we will usually project this disdain onto people who exhibit these same characteristics in order to further distance ourselves from our own shadow.

In the world of psychotherapy, there is an approach called Internal Family Systems (IFS). In fact, the creator of IFS, Richard Schwartz, has acknowledged that the work of Jung heavily influenced the creation of IFS. The IFS model suggests that our minds are made up of a community of parts, each with its own perspective and purpose. Parts work is like being in a work meeting where everyone has a voice, and everyone wants what's best for the project, even if their approach might differ or even be chaotic at times.

In IFS, there is a concept called "the Self." We will be exploring this concept throughout this book, and you may notice that "Self" is always capitalized. This is to distinguish it as the core of who you are—a calm, compassionate, and understanding presence within you. It's like the director of a play, overseeing an entire production. The Self is curious, nonjudgmental, and accepting of all of our parts. It's that wise, intuitive voice that can guide us through difficult times. Shadow work is essentially a personal quest for self-realization, epitomizing the journey toward feeling like this authentic, compassionate Self within the framework of IFS.

The shadow is similar to the concept of the exile part within the IFS framework. Exiles are parts of us that carry our emotional pain or unmet needs based on past experiences. Exiles tend to be hidden or suppressed in order to avoid reexperiencing the pain associated with them. However, if left unattended, these exiles can influence our thoughts, emotions, and behaviors in negative ways—much like the shadow can.

Just like our shadow can emerge without warning, so can our exiles. When this happens, our protective parts, known as managers and firefighters in the IFS framework, show up and do whatever they can to help the exile evade pain and discomfort. This process is similar to our shadow functioning as a form of self-repression or projection.

In *Psychological Aspects of the Personality*, Jung said, "Everything that irritates us about others can lead us to an understanding of ourselves." In this context, Jung is referring to the psychological concept of projection, where we assign our own unconscious thoughts, feelings, and motivations to others. We may even feel resentful that other people are behaving, engaging in, or existing in ways that we wish we could but feel the need to hide. Jung believed that by recognizing these projections, we can gain deeper insights into our own inner world, leading to a greater capacity for self-awareness and understanding of others. (We will explore this more in Chapter 3.)

For example, growing up you may have been a child who was curious and asked a lot of questions. However, perhaps a caregiver, teacher, or other figure of authority in your life reprimanded you for asking "too many questions." Or maybe you were made to feel "dumb" or "silly" for the types of questions you asked. The curious nature of your personality may then have felt the need to be repressed in order to keep you safe from future embarrassment or shame. Now as an adult you may avoid asking questions altogether and try to figure everything out on your own. You may even begrudge the people around you who ask a lot of questions.

Now imagine you are driving and another vehicle suddenly cuts in front of you. Instantly, you are enraged, muttering about how entitled this person is. Maybe you even shout expletives or lay on the horn to express your disapproval. But if you pause and ask yourself why this behavior triggers such a strong reaction, you might uncover some uncomfortable truths about yourself. If it's the driver's sense of entitlement that angers you to the point of intense reactivity, it could be a sign that you, too, possess traits of entitlement that you have not acknowledged. Of course, there is a fine line between reacting to genuinely reckless or inappropriate behavior and recognizing when a shadow aspect of yourself is being projected. Not every reaction we have is indicative of a shadow, but it's worth being curious about. The point here is that by becoming enraged by this behavior, we are unconsciously creating distance between the behavior that reflects our shadow and persona (the image we present to the world). We will do whatever we can to avoid being associated with our shadow material.

Shadow work is the act of shining a gentle light on these very aspects of ourselves that we try to keep hidden, the parts that fuel feelings of insecurity, low self-esteem, and diminished self-worth. But why would we want to shine a light onto what we believe are "unfavorable" parts of ourselves? Because without fully exploring every aspect of who we are as complex beings, we can't fully become who we want to be. It's within this quest for balance that we discover the innate value and resilience within us, even among the shadows we contain.

Jung believed it was necessary to acknowledge and invite the shadow into our conscious awareness in order to feel whole and authentic. So, in essence, shadow work is about inviting the shadow to have a seat at the table—maybe for the very first time. First-time guests can feel a bit awkward, so there is usually a need to be patient with yourself and your shadows as well.

An important concept to incorporate into this process is radical acceptance, which involves acknowledging the reality of a situation without trying to change it. Radical acceptance is the recognition that certain things are beyond our control, and instead of resisting or fighting against them, we choose to accept them as they are. This does not mean we condone these behaviors or traits, or agree with them; it just means we accept that certain experiences have happened (or in this case, certain shadows were formed) and focus on how we respond to it. Shadow work is similar in that this work is not about condoning or embracing these traits as acceptable, but rather about working to understand their origin, when they become activated, and the stories they create, so that they no longer control us unconsciously.

Becoming acquainted with our shadow deepens our relationship not only with ourselves but also with others. As we engage in shadow work, we become less reactive and more compassionate, empathetic, and understanding. This process helps us recognize that the traits we once despised in others may actually be reflections of our own unacknowledged parts that deserve attention. As we explore these hidden parts, our conversations with ourselves and others become more meaningful, providing clarity about why we think, feel, and behave the way we do. At the same time, we create space to accept and feel more at peace with life's inherent ambiguity.

HISTORICAL AND PSYCHOLOGICAL PERSPECTIVES OF THE SHADOW

Carl Jung's work on identifying the shadow originated from his exploration of the collective unconscious, which can be described as a vast reservoir of universally shared experiences and archetypal symbols that help shape our individual psyches. Essentially, the collective unconscious is a container of memories, symbols, and experiences inherited from our ancestors, which influence our behaviors and perceptions.

Before Jung's theories on the shadow emerged, he was working alongside Sigmund Freud, who had developed his own theories on the unconscious mind where he specifically identified the id, ego, and superego. In Freud's framework, the id represents the impulsive part of our personality, which is driven by pleasure and avoids pain. The id is the raw, instinctual part within us. The superego, on the other hand, is the judgmental and morally correct aspect of our personality, constantly striving for perfection and wanting us to adhere to societal norms. Freud believed the ego served as the conscious mediator between the id and the superego by balancing the demands of the both of them. In Freud's view, the ego's job is to navigate the complexities of reality and decision-making.

Freud's theory of the id and Jung's theory of the shadow differ in that Freud believed the unconscious, repressed parts of ourselves (the id) were driven by primal urges. Jung, however, believed our unconscious shadow was made up of the parts of ourselves that we repressed or denied because they were deemed unfavorable by others.

From a historical perspective, the concept of the shadow has roots that extend beyond the work of Jung and Freud. In *The Origins and History of Consciousness*, Erich Neumann acknowledges that the existence of a "dark side" within humanity has been recognized for centuries through cultural, artistic, and religious explorations. Neumann goes on to explore this further in his book *Depth Psychology and a New Ethic*, where he theorized that collective devastation was inevitable when we ignore, repress, or project our shadows onto others, because it leads to division and detachment. Neumann believed that by acknowledging our personal and collective shadows, we could experience a sense of wholeness, which would also increase our capacity for curiosity, compassion, and empathy for ourselves and the experiences of others. This collective perspective highlights the importance of shadow work, not only for personal growth but also for the well-being of society because it encourages us to confront what we metaphorically see in the mirror, on an individual and societal level.

When we grant ourselves permission to step into the world of our personal and collective shadow, we are able to access the subconscious, which is the holding space for our deepest fears, anxieties, shame, etc. This can be a place we are conditioned to avoid because while stepping into it can be enlightening and magickal, it's also formidable.

EXERCISE: THE PSYCHOANALYTIC SHADOW SPREAD

Given the importance of these internal structures in shaping our psyche, we can use the theories of Jung, Freud, and Neumann to explore the shadow, along with the help of tarot. This tarot spread helps to explore the interplay of the id, ego, and superego, while also integrating the process of shadow work. While using tarot can be a beneficial tool for this exercise, reflection through journaling can also reveal enlightening information.

Begin by shuffling a card for each prompt below. Card 1 will be your anchor card representing a potential shadow, while cards 2 through 5 help you answer the reflection questions posed. See the example for more guidance.

Card 1: Shadow Awareness. In what ways do you identify with this archetype as a potential shadow?

Card 2: Shadow in Relationships. How does this shadow (card 1) manifest in your relationships with yourself and others?

Card 3: The Id. What subconscious motivations drive your impulses as they relate to this shadow?

Card 4: The Superego. What personality traits help regulate and keep your primal shadow impulses in check?

Card 5: The Ego. How does your conscious Self balance inner primal urges (card 3) with logic and moral reasoning (card 4)?

❧ *Reflect* ❧

Here is an example reading.

Card 1: The High Priestess (see Chapter 5 for shadow archetype descriptions). As a shadow, the High Priestess can be avoidant, reject opportunities for self-reflection, and withhold valuable information.

Card 2: Ace of Cups. This card typically represents an overflow and abundance of love and care. However, with the High Priestess as the shadow, the experience of abundance with the Ace of Cups is inaccessible as the High Priestess's avoidance limits connection with others, thus limiting their ability to receive care and feel fulfilled.

Card 3: The Nine of Swords. This card represents the subconscious motivation of "worst case scenario" thinking to protect the Self from getting hurt, which drives the impulse of the High Priestess's shadow to withhold information from others to avoid getting too close and potentially getting hurt.

Card 4: The Emperor. This card could help regulate the impulses of the shadow by keeping that part accountable and asking direct, confronting questions such as "What are your intentions?" or "In what way does your behavior help and/or hinder me?"

Card 5: Knight of Pentacles. This card mediates between these two forces (cards 3 and 4) by holding space for the vulnerability of the Nine of Swords without being overtaken by it. It also helps with integrating the Emperor's authority without losing sight of reality. The Knight of Pentacles takes everything into account before moving forward with confidence.

SHADOW FORMATION

Shadow formation is deeply connected to shame. Researcher and social worker Brené Brown has explored shame extensively, describing it as a powerful and isolating force that contributes to a "fear of disconnection." In her research, Brown found that individuals frequently suppress the parts of themselves they believe others would find undesirable (which is exactly what happens with the shadow). As humans, we crave connection so it would make sense that anything that could potentially threaten that need for connection, such as a behavior or personality trait, would then be repressed for the sake of continued safety and communal and societal acceptance. This theory aligns with Jungian concepts of the shadow, where it becomes a container of traits, desires, or impulses that remain suppressed due to fear of social consequences.

Archetypes, like those represented in the tarot, can serve as powerful tools for self-exploration, particularly when it comes to shadow work and shame because they can help us uncover and integrate hidden aspects of ourselves. We will explore the Major Arcana, as well as the four tarot suits, as reflections of the shadow in Chapter 5. However, we can turn to the court cards in tarot when thinking about shadow formation, specifically the Pages. From a developmental perspective, the Pages are deeply connected to childhood and adolescence (key periods when our shadows begin to form). The rest of the court cards, the Knights, Queens, and Kings, are also pivotal archetypal markers of development to explore when considering shadow formation throughout the lifespan as they can represent early, middle, and late adulthood, respectively.

During the formative years of our childhood, we collect experiences that inevitably shape our understanding of ourselves and the world around us. We develop traits, habits, and coping mechanisms in response to the experiences, expectations, and limitations imposed on us by society, care-givers, and peers. During this time, certain aspects of our personality may be labeled as undesirable by people we consider important. As a result, we learn to suppress these traits, which then become part of our shadow.

The Pages in tarot reflect this critical stage of life, where curiosity and innocence meet external challenges and expectations. Each Page represents a specific aspect of development. By engaging with these archetypes, we can revisit our own developmental experiences, allowing us to explore where our shadows may have formed and how they continue to influence our behaviors and perceptions as adults.

For example, the Page of Cups embodies the shadow of being told we are "too emotional" or "too sensitive." This type of messaging can create a disconnection from our true feelings and establish an internalized belief that vulnerability is a weakness, creating a shadow that stifles authentic emotional expression and awareness. Additionally, this can create a shadow that looks like a lack of empathy for others, especially if anger and frustration are experienced when witnessing the authentic emotions of others.

With the Page of Swords, a shadow can form when our ideas are dismissed or our intelligence is questioned. For example, being told that our thoughts are silly can lead to a shadow where self-doubt thrives, which ends up limiting our willingness to express ourself or engage intellectually with others. This shadow can also be marked by rigidity and feeling as though our ideas are better than others' and dismissing anything that doesn't align with our own ways of thinking and processing.

The Page of Wands might indicate experiencing the formation of a shadow in relation to being labeled as "too much"—too talkative, too inquisitive, or too enthusiastic. These judgments can lead to a suppression of curiosity and creativity, creating a shadow where we feel the need to hold back our natural excitement, desires, and goals. This shadow can also include feeling inconvenienced by, or envious of, others' joy and self-expression.

The Page of Pentacles embodies the shadow of being deemed irresponsible or inadequate, especially in regards to practical tasks, chores, and executive functioning. Alternatively, excessive praise for always completing tasks perfectly can instill a sense of perfectionism. Both scenarios lead to a shadow that can undermine the confidence in our ability to navigate the world as an adult. This shadow can also be marked by feeling as though our way is the right and only way, limiting the space and ability for others to share their own unique process and perspective.

EXERCISE: PAGES OF THE PAST

Begin by laying out each of the Pages from your tarot deck and reflect on how their shadow elements from the descriptions above resonate with your own experiences. After contemplation, shuffle your deck and pull a card to accompany the Page that resonates with you most. This accompanying card represents the voice of that Page's shadow. Through reflective dialogue with these cards, consider what insights they reveal.

REFLECT

- What does the card you pulled want you to understand about the Page's shadow?

- How might this Page express its needs, fears, or words of wisdom if it could speak directly to you?

PAGES OF THE PAST: IN ACTION

In our sessions, one client found themself frequently receiving feedback from both partners and colleagues about their tendency toward rigidity and inflexibility. These patterns had created subtle fractures in their relationships, leaving others feeling unseen, unheard, and disconnected. Through reflection, the client felt a strong identification with the Page of Pentacles, which led us to explore underlying childhood traumas—experiences steeped in shame and hypervigilance. For them, the Page of Pentacles became a powerful symbol of a wounded shadow self.

While working through this exercise, the client pulled the Ten of Wands to accompany their Page of Pentacles shadow. The Ten of Wands, symbolizing feeling burdened and overextended, brought to light the emotional and psychological load that had developed from years of striving for perfection and control in order to feel safe. The Ten of Wands acted as a mirror, reflecting how their perfectionistic tendencies had become not just a habit but a burden that weighed heavily on their self-expression and ability to connect with others. This card allowed the client to dialogue about what it would be like to create space that allowed others to take on some of the responsibilities they had been unnecessarily carrying and showed the client that they are still safe, even if they are not always in control.

THE GOLDEN SHADOW

While the overarching theme of the shadow and shadow work generally encompasses what we might consider "undesirable" traits or characteristics, Jungian analysts and enthusiasts have also gone on to coin the term "golden shadow," which acknowledges positive qualities and traits such as our creativity, curiosity, or even our sense of humor that may have been dismissed or ignored by others—giving us the impression that we should deny or repress these parts of ourselves.

Because the shadow acts as a container of traits we believe to be "negative," the golden shadow then functions as a container of our repressed potential and authenticity. Golden shadow work is equally as important and valuable as any other form of shadow work.

Information about our own golden shadows can often be discovered in moments of admiration and awe of others in the same way that aspects of our shadow can be found in moments of judgment of others. Think about the last time you said something like "Wow, you're incredible. I could never do something like that." Our golden shadow is usually hiding in the places where we are easily able to praise others, but quick to put ourselves down or deny that those same characteristics or skills could, or do, exist within us.

Another way to explore the golden shadow is to think about what you feel like you are supposed to be humble and modest about. Perhaps you are afraid you will look like you are bragging if you talk about that incredible art piece you have been working on in secret. Maybe you are scared to let people see your extensive vinyl collection because you don't want them to judge your special interest or what you spend your money on. Or maybe you have a knack for public speaking but have always been told to avoid the spotlight so as not to seem arrogant or self-centered. Reflecting on these areas where you have downplayed your talents or passions allows you to uncover aspects of your golden shadow.

So, in essence, if our shadow parts reflect what we do not want to be, then the golden shadow parts reflect what we wish we could be. The golden shadow contains those hidden strengths and personal joys that, when acknowledged, can bring deeper fulfillment and confidence into our life.

Uncovering the Golden Shadow with Tarot: A Case Study

I once worked with a client who had a loose tarot practice. They would occasionally pull cards, but their primary interest lay in discussing archetypal symbols and how they related to their personal experiences. In sessions, the client frequently used tarot language to describe their emotional states, often saying things like "I was having a High Priestess moment this weekend," or "I'm feeling incredibly Five of Cups this week." These conversations provided a shared symbolic framework that enriched our therapeutic dialogue, creating a unique, shared language between us.

As we explored issues related to self-esteem and assertiveness, the concept of the shadow surfaced in one session. The client was already familiar with several aspects of their shadow but felt stuck in their progress toward greater confidence. I introduced the concept of the golden shadow, and the client was immediately intrigued.

In situations where clients bring tarot into therapy sessions, I often allow them to take the lead. This particular session was no different. The client, eager and energized by the prospect of discovering new facets of their psyche, began shuffling their deck with palpable excitement. There was no set spread or specific prompt—just the client, their deck, and the intention to explore. When they pulled the card, however, their enthusiasm waned. It was the Five of Pentacles, a card traditionally associated with hardship, adversity, and feelings of being unsupported.

The client's body language shifted immediately. Sensing their disappointment, I encouraged them to share what they were feeling in response to the card. They expressed frustration, having hoped for a card with a more positive or empowering message. After giving them a moment to reflect, I guided the conversation toward the golden shadow concept. Instead of focusing on the traditional meaning of the card, I asked, "What untapped potential might exist within you based on this archetype?"

This reframing of the card sparked a renewed sense of engagement. The client began to reflect on their strengths, specifically their ability to navigate challenging situations and "figure it out" when life became difficult. They recognized that a significant part of their golden shadow involved an innate ability to find solutions, a skill they had developed but often overlooked due to its association with being in survival mode. The conversation deepened as they recalled memories of being labeled as "bossy" in childhood for directing others, a label that caused them to suppress this part of their personality. However, they began to see this trait as an underacknowledged strength that could be further cultivated by giving themselves permission to take the lead at work or with friends by suggesting new restaurants or activities.

Through this process, the Five of Pentacles—initially seen as a symbol of struggle—became a mirror reflecting the client's hidden strengths and untapped potential. This experience highlighted the value of archetypal imagery in helping individuals identify parts of themselves that have been denied or repressed, illustrating how tarot can serve as a powerful tool in uncovering and integrating aspects of the shadow and the golden shadow. It's also a lesson in not taking tarot so literally, especially when using it as a tool for personal healing and self-discovery.

When Others Find Your Golden Shadow: A (Personal) Case Study

Sometimes it's not even us who identifies our own shadow. Sometimes it's a friend, colleague, or partner who shines a light on the parts of us we have pushed away. A friend and fellow tarot practitioner, Amanda (Mandy) Hughes, wrote the book *Mystic Storyteller: A Writer's Guide to Using the Tarot for Creative Inspiration* and created a companion tarot deck to go along with it. During the deck creation process, she reached out and told me she had a surprise for me. In her Mystic Storyteller Tarot deck, she had made me the Queen of Pentacles.

There on her wood carved throne, laptop in lap, black chunky glasses, purple streaked hair, and witchy boots was me, as the Queen of Pentacles. When I say I sobbed, I mean it was messy. It was an undeniable honor to be included in such a significant project, but what Mandy did not realize was that she just unearthed one of my shadows—a golden shadow.

I have always identified with the Queen of Swords, which might seem counterintuitive to being a therapist since the Queen of Swords is an archetype often known to be cold and rigid. However, there are many traits of hers that I have embodied in order to stay safe throughout my life, including her ability to set and maintain strict boundaries and unapologetically share her truth. She feels like a warrior whose motto is probably "Do no harm, but take no shit."

The Queen of Pentacles, on the other hand, is an archetype I always associated with a very dear friend of mine, Jane. I met Jane in 2018, which somehow feels like a lifetime ago and just yesterday at the same time. I had moved in across the street from her and her husband and not one week into being a first-time homeowner, I lost my entire savings because anything and everything that could have broken or gone wrong did.

The first time Jane introduced herself to me was when I was wrapping up a conversation with the fifth company specializing in some sort of home catastrophe repair work. She walked over and in the kindest, warmest, most comforting British accent said, "Sweetheart, what's been going on? There is always a repairman here." I wanted to reach out and hug this woman out of a pure instinctual drive, and I nearly did. Her Queen of Pentacles energy was palpable, and I had to stop myself from collapsing into her.

My relationship with Jane, my Queen of Pentacles, began at that exact moment and turned into weekly morning coffee and donut dates, Sunday brunches, and Saturday game nights where we would stay up until two in the morning playing vintage board games and laughing about the absurdities of life.

Jane's home is always spotless despite having multiple cats and dogs. She will make you a cup of coffee, feed you donuts and pastries, and ask you about life, love, and self-care. She will ask if you are taking enough walks and taking breaks from work, but also if you have read that recent article about growing your business or getting a raise. She may even offer you some "medicinal oils" with your coffee.

She is the Queen of Pentacles I always wanted and needed, but certainly not the archetype I would associate with myself. So when Mandy surprised me with my likeness as the Queen of Pentacles in her deck, I had a plethora of feelings to process. I was balancing feelings of honor and joy with fear, imposter syndrome, and even embarrassment. I admired Jane for exuding the energy of the Queen of Pentacles, and for someone else to view me similarly felt wrong.

Often, golden shadows are hiding in the spaces we feel we are supposed to be humble and modest. I love taking care of people, but, as a golden shadow, I don't want to be recognized for it. My thoughts say, "Of course this is who I am, and this is what I am supposed to be doing. This is where my worth and my value lie, so there is nothing special about it."

In her book, Mandy describes the Queen of Pentacles as "grounded, solid, unwavering, and dependable. Like their Page and Knight counterparts, this Queen is steady, resolute, consistent, and persistent in their endeavors. They dedicate all of their time and effort to the supportive role they play in their home and work environments—and work, they most certainly do."

Mandy's description of the Queen of Pentacles resonates deeply with me, yet I can feel a physical resistance within me—a sense that my shadow is shutting down, almost like it's covering its ears and saying, "Nope. Don't go there. Stop talking about it." This internal voice and sensation are precisely what we need to tune into during shadow work, especially golden shadow work, as it is what reveals the hidden material we need to explore in order to uncover our shadows and deepen our self-awareness and self-compassion.

EXERCISE: IDENTIFYING THE GOLDEN SHADOW

To explore the golden shadow, we can reflect on the prompts below or pull tarot cards to help us access our unconscious and provide more depth to our discoveries.

Card 1: My unacknowledged potential

Card 2: An obstacle preventing me from embracing this potential

Card 3: A way I can reclaim and integrate this hidden potential into my life

⇒ *Reflect* ⇐

IDENTIFYING THE GOLDEN SHADOW IN ACTION

In this exercise, we will continue exploring the Queen of Pentacles as a golden shadow and pull cards to help explore this golden shadow further. You may choose to intentionally pull a card that represents qualities others have identified in you or that you admire in others. Or you could shuffle and intuitively pull a card to explore how it could represent your own golden shadow.

Card 1: The Queen of Pentacles embodies a warm, nurturing presence, grounded in reliability and an instinctual drive to care for others. This archetype is always looking for ways to help others create, find, and make the most of their resources, while also being generous with their own time and resources. With the Queen of Pentacles, they are all about finding ways to make life a little easier and a little more comfortable for everyone around them.

Card 2: The King of Cups archetype represents emotional maturity, control, and balance. However, as an obstacle, it can suggest a struggle with these qualities, leading to emotional suppression and denial of golden shadow qualities. This suppression can manifest in the form of a defense mechanism, preventing us from acknowledging and celebrating the qualities of the Queen of Pentacles others see in her. By denying the opportunity to experience being seen as the Queen of Pentacles, we inadvertently diminish the importance of our ability to provide nurturance and support to others and, in turn, diminish the connection other folks have been able to experience with us. Essentially, the King of Cups as an obstacle represents the dismissive nature of our response to this golden shadow, seeing it as merely fulfilling an expected role rather than recognizing it as a valued strength and quality.

Card 3: The Ace of Wands archetype is a fierce card to represent ways to reclaim and integrate the hidden potential of the Queen of Pentacles into our life. The Ace of Wands is buzzing with proactive energy, fueled by excitement and creativity. With the Queen of Pentacles being the epitome of resourcefulness and the Ace of Wands representing the energy of creation, it seems as though the suggestion here is to approach our unacknowledged potential as a form of art. Art is inherently subjective and viewing the golden shadow of the Queen of Pentacles as subjective art gives it room to expand and contract, which naturally takes away some of the pressure of perfectionism so many of us are prone to.

What cards have you pulled?

Card 1: _____

Thoughts: _____

_____

_____

Card 2: _____

Thoughts: _____

_____

_____

Card 3: _____

Thoughts: _____

_____

_____

Chapter 3

Shadow Dynamics
and Mental Health

❧

The most fundamental aggression to ourselves,
the most fundamental harm we can do to ourselves,
is to remain ignorant by not having the courage and respect
to look at ourselves honestly and gently.

—PEMA CHÖDRÖN

THE SHADOW IN OUR THOUGHTS, FEELINGS, AND BEHAVIORS

Acknowledging and eventually integrating the shadow allow us to be both self-aware and self-accepting, the latter of which can be a difficult and life-long journey for many of us. When we are not self-aware and the shadow is not integrated, we unconsciously act out based on the material of our shadows because the shadow manifests in a variety of subtle and covert ways. This manifestation can look like defensiveness, where we react strongly to criticism or feedback, or projecting the parts of ourselves we do not want to acknowledge onto others. Or it could sound like judgmental thoughts toward others, where we judge traits in them that we secretly fear or dislike in ourselves but might not yet be aware of.

An unexamined shadow can halt our personal growth, sabotage romantic and platonic relationships, hinder our happiness, and limit our potential because the shadow influences our thoughts, emotions, behaviors, and relationship dynamics. However, as we engage in shadow work and navigate the process of coming to know all parts of ourselves, we become more aware of our thoughts, feelings, and behaviors and how they connect to different parts of our psyche. It's during this experience that we gain a heightened sensitivity to the subtle cues and manifestations of our shadow parts. It is similar to our eyes finally starting to adjust to a dark or dimly lit room. After a few minutes, we start to see things more clearly and we start to feel more comfortable navigating the space even though it's still dark. We are no longer walking around with our arms outstretched carefully feeling for things we might bump into, because now we have the ability to see the outlines of furniture and can understand where our bodies exist within the darkness.

As we venture into the world of the shadow, we may notice recurring themes in our thoughts, such as persistent self-criticisms or judgments of ourselves and others. We may even discover hidden talents or interests that may have been stifled (this is the golden shadow emerging). Similarly, our behaviors may reveal unconscious motivations or unresolved conflicts that influence our interactions with others and the world around us.

Our shadow parts can emerge without warning and when they do, it can feel absolutely destabilizing, especially when they have gone unacknowledged up until this point. A sense of injustice, an unmet need, an unhealed pain point, or a violation of a boundary could send the shadow-self spiraling. It is in these reactionary moments that we need to dig around and see what has not yet been tended to. When we have not spent time exploring these repressed emotions, they will often arise from a place of reactivity, which can be harmful to ourselves and our relationships. These types of emotions serve as valuable indicators of the possible presence of shadow material, offering insights into hidden wounds, unmet needs, and unresolved traumas. Feelings of anger, resentment, jealousy, or shame may highlight areas of our psyche that require attention, compassion, and curiosity as we engage in shadow work.

To better explain this concept, we can look at the therapeutic modality of Cognitive Behavioral Therapy (CBT). This framework focuses on the idea that core beliefs give rise to automatic thoughts, which in turn influence emotions and behaviors. While intrusive thoughts, automatic negative thoughts, or negative core beliefs are not always linked to or associated with one of our shadows, understanding these experiences can help us better understand how our shadows and the material they hold function. Within the framework of CBT, these automatic thoughts are often associated with cognitive distortions—irrational or biased thought patterns that reinforce negative beliefs about ourselves. There are plenty of criticisms of CBT, and I have plenty of my own (as it's not the ideal therapeutic modality for everyone). However, concepts within this framework are helpful to identify patterns in our thinking, especially when we are exploring the shadow. When we can identify these patterns, we increase our self-awareness. (Do note, however, that a modality like CBT is not recommended when exploring thoughts or feelings around traumatic events.)

Some of the most common cognitive distortions I see in my practice are:

- **All-or-Nothing Thinking:** Viewing situations in black-and-white terms, or seeing things as either perfect or awful, with no middle ground or willingness to acknowledge a "gray" area.

- **Overgeneralization:** Generalizing a single negative event to an overall pattern, leading to negative self-assessment and worldview.

- **Mental Filter:** Focusing on a single negative detail while ignoring positive aspects, leading to a pessimistic perspective.

- **Magical Thinking:** Making negative predictions about the future without sufficient evidence, treating them as facts. Believing we know what others are thinking, often assuming negative thoughts without evidence.

- **Catastrophizing:** Exaggerating the importance of negative events or minimizing positive achievements, skewing perspective.

- **Emotional Reasoning:** Accepting emotions as facts or believing that feeling something makes it true.

- **Should Statements:** Imposing unrealistic expectations on ourselves or others, leading to guilt and shame.

- **Labeling:** Assigning negative labels to ourselves or others based on a single event, often using emotionally charged language.

- **Personalization:** Blaming oneself for events beyond one's control, assuming undue responsibility for others' feelings and actions.

These cognitive distortions are closely tied to core beliefs. For instance, if a person holds a core belief of "I'm unlovable," they may engage in all-or-nothing thinking when a romantic relationship ends, believing that they are completely unworthy of love from anyone. This can lead to feelings of despair and self-isolation that cause them to struggle in believing that someone could truly love them. The behavior of self-isolation then limits their ability to connect with others, which can validate the cognitive distortion and core belief that they are unlovable. This is how a self-fulfilling prophecy takes root and how, without adequate self-reflection, this type of self-fulfilling prophecy can significantly impact the quality of our lives.

This cycle can influence a person's perceptions, decisions, and actions. For example, someone with a core belief of "I'm a failure," or "I'm never good enough," may engage in avoidant behaviors due to the fear of failing, thus limiting their opportunities for success. This avoidance then leads to fewer accomplishments, which then reinforces the original belief of being a failure.

How does the shadow play into this example, then? The shadow might emerge when a person with this core belief, engaging in this cognitive distortion, finds themself envious or critical of the success of others. Because they believe they are incapable, seeing other people put forth effort to succeed triggers their own shadow around this experience.

In these instances, there is usually a response or reaction tied to an emotion we aren't comfortable with, so we have to identify the emotion, explore the reaction, and then work to get comfortable expressing the unmet need, boundary violation, or pain point that was triggered in the first place. Knowing and implementing all of this are what helps us feel balanced and regulated and one step closer to feeling integrated and whole.

Much like identifying core beliefs, when we set aside time or make space for our shadows to speak or tell their own story, we can help uncover the hidden causes and underlying dynamics of our discomfort and reactivity. Spending time with the shadow allows us to discover where it's rooted and that information helps us to figure out healthier ways to express this without suppressing the original emotion.

• • •

Take a moment to reflect on your own core beliefs and how they interact with any cognitive distortions you may have. When do you notice these cognitive distortions becoming activated? In what ways might they be linked to a shadow?

EXERCISE: COGNITIVE DISTORTION SPREAD

Review the list of cognitive distortions above. Choose a cognitive distortion that you feel you experience, then follow the spread instructions below.

Card 1: Choose a card that you feel represents the cognitive distortion you experience.

Now pull for the next five cards.

Card 2: When does this cognitive distortion appear in your life the most?

Card 3: Where did this cognitive distortion originate?

Card 4: What shadow may be linked to this cognitive distortion?

Card 5: How might you work to manage this cognitive distortion?

Card 6: How will this impact the shadow it is linked to?

⇒ *Reflect* ⇐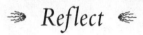

The cards for my Cognitive Distortion Exercise are:

Card 1: _____

Thoughts: _____

_____

Card 2: _____

Thoughts: _____

_____

Card 3: _____

Thoughts: _____

_____

Card 4: _____

Thoughts: _____

_____

Card 5: _____

Thoughts: _____

_____

Card 6: _____

Thoughts: _____

_____

THE SHADOW IN PSYCHOTHERAPY

I was working with a client who vehemently despised their college class-mates to the point where it was impacting their ability to function in class. The sudden onset of these feelings had me curious about what might be happening below this client's level of awareness. So we spent some time discussing the behaviors of the people this client disliked (gossiping, exclusion, etc.), and eventually uncovered personal shame the client felt for having treated others this same way in the past and realizing they had the capacity to behave similarly.

The client now held themself to a higher standard in terms of how they interact with others, which was in direct conflict with how they had acted in the past. The client had buried this part of themself for many years, hoping to never speak of it again due to the intense shame it brought them. However, this newfound disdain for their classmates was poking at this buried shadow and causing it to bubble up to the surface. The intense frustration this client felt toward their classmates was now also being felt toward themself. We spent several sessions unwrapping the behaviors the client felt shame around—exploring all of the necessary whys and hows while also infusing the conversation with radical acceptance.

Radical acceptance is a tool used within the framework of Dialectical Behavior Therapy (DBT) where we acknowledge that we can't change the past and we may not even condone it, but we can accept that it happened, and we take accountability for how we react and respond in the aftermath of the situation. Through the discovery of the client's shadow, along with the infusion of radical acceptance, self-forgiveness, and compassion, the client was able to feel less stressed and anxious going to class. They realized that by acknowledging that they too have the capacity to engage in similar behaviors, it gave them a sense of freedom. Their fear of exposing the shadow was what was amplifying the feelings of anger and anxiety. Giving the shadow space to coexist and merely acknowledge its existence meant the client was no longer so strongly distracted or triggered by those same behaviors of their classmates.

➺ *Reflect* ➻

Jung theorized that our own shadows are often reflected in the behaviors and characteristics we most frequently criticize in others. Use the prompts below to help you identify that which you judge in others. You may choose to pull tarot cards to help you access unconscious material.

In what ways are you judgmental, harsh, or critical of others?

_____

_____

_____

_____

How might these criticisms of others reflect a personal shadow you have?

_____

_____

_____

_____

What might this shadow need in order to feel safe working toward integration?

_____

_____

_____

_____

THE EGO

To fully understand the shadow and appreciate the depths of shadow work, it's important to also understand the role of the ego and its relationship with the shadow. Jung described the ego as the representation of our conscious mind, acting as the container of our thoughts and the center of our consciousness. The ego helps us navigate our surroundings and encompasses everything we understand about ourselves. By organizing all of our identities, the ego enables us to make sense of our thoughts, feelings, and experiences, ultimately providing us with a coherent sense of Self.

The ego plays a critical role in decision-making as well by helping us evaluate situations, weighing options, and helping us choose responses based on our goals and values. It also plays a role in our relationships by helping us to communicate effectively, assert ourselves, and respond appropriately to social situations. In this way, the ego acts as a buffer between our inner desires and the expectations of the outside world, facilitating a delicate balance between our basic needs and desires and our moral standards and societal norms. Unfortunately, despite these vital functions, the ego often receives an unfair reputation in popular culture, where it is frequently conflated with selfishness.

The relationship between the ego and the shadow is delicate. When the ego denies or suppresses the existence of the shadow, it inadvertently increases the shadow's desire for control. This denial can lead to the shadow gaining power over the ego's thoughts, ultimately influencing our behaviors. For instance, an ego that prides itself on rationality and logical thinking may struggle with intense emotional dysregulation or develop harsh judgments toward more sensitive individuals when the shadow is activated. This tendency highlights the importance of recognizing and integrating the shadow, in order to foster healthier, more balanced relationships not just with others but also with the ego.

In addition to Freud and Jung, other prominent figures in the world of psychology, such as Erik Erikson, Carl Rogers, and Karen Horney, have also developed theories on the role of the ego. Erikson, for example, emphasized the ego's critical role in shaping and maintaining a cohesive self-identity throughout the lifespan. His stages of psychosocial development suggest that the ego is responsible for resolving conflicts at each stage of human development, making it a crucial component in navigating these challenges. In this context, the ego becomes a vital collaborator when engaging in shadow work, as it helps integrate and balance various aspects of the Self.

Similar to Erikson's theories, psychologist Carl Rogers also placed significant emphasis on the role of the ego in psychological growth and development, though his focus was more on personal fulfillment and self-actualization. Rogers believed that the ego is essential for achieving self-actualization, a state in which an individual's true Self aligns with their ideal Self. He theorized that the ego strives for internal and external congruence, meaning that individuals are driven by the desire to feel authentic and whole, both within themselves and in their interactions with the outside world.

Psychoanalyst Karen Horney's view of the ego emphasized the role of social and cultural factors in shaping personality. She believed the ego is primarily responsible for managing the basic anxiety that arises from interpersonal relationships and societal pressures. In response to external pressures, Horney believed the ego develops defense strategies to cope, such as seeking approval, exerting control, or withdrawing from others. These defenses, while protective, can also distort the individual's self-perception, making the ego a potential obstacle in shadow work, as it prevents self-awareness and limits integration of the shadow aspects of the Self.

THE PERSONA

Another important aspect of the psyche that is important to understand as it relates to the shadow is the concept of the persona. The persona represents the social mask we wear to adhere to societal expectations; it is a source of protection acting as our unique approach to navigating and responding to the world around us. While essential for navigating daily life, the persona often obscures the hidden aspects of the Self (such as the shadow) by repressing qualities that may not align with an acceptable social image. We can extend this concept further by examining how art and archetypes help us identify our persona and explore its impact in shadow work.

At the onset of my career, I worked extensively with children and families affected by trauma. One of the most impactful interventions I used with children was rooted in art therapy—specifically, the creation of masks. These children, having endured unspeakable violence and profound emotional distress, often struggled to find the words to describe their inner pain. They were trapped in a space where their external and internal realities were at odds, lacking the language to bridge the gap between what they felt, what they experienced, and what they expressed.

Art became an essential tool in facilitating this connection. Mask-making, in particular, served as a nonthreatening and accessible medium that allowed children to explore their emotional landscapes. In its simplest form, I would provide my young clients with a sheet of paper, asking them to depict an "outside mask" on one side—representing how they presented themselves to the world. On the reverse side, they would draw or write what this external mask concealed—their hidden emotions, fears, worries, and internal experiences. This exercise offered them a tangible way to access and understand their emotions, bridging the dissonance between their inner and outer worlds.

I expanded this exercise for older kids and teenagers, incorporating actual masks and a variety of mixed media materials, transforming it into a more immersive and symbolic process. This progression from simple sketches to intricate mask-making deepened the therapeutic experience, allowing my clients to articulate complex emotions they had previously been unable to express. I share this experience because the therapeutic intervention of mask-making mirrors the concept of the persona as theorized by Jung.

We have to be careful to not overidentify with our persona, as doing so can disconnect us from our core Self and create emotional distance in personal relationships. When we become too rigidly attached to the social mask we wear in public, it can become difficult to shift between our public and private selves. If this concept sounds familiar, it's because as a society, our social media personalities function similarly to the concept of the persona. It can be incredibly difficult to separate our social media persona from our core Self. In tarot, this dynamic can be illustrated through the Queen of Swords. Often depicted as sharp, critical, and well-boundaried, this archetype serves a valuable purpose in protecting our emotions and vulnerabilities in the outside world. However, when someone overidentifies with the Queen of Swords persona, they may struggle to drop the sword in their personal life, keeping their loved ones at a distance. This inability to reveal a softer, more vulnerable side can inhibit the formation of deep and meaningful connections with partners, children, friends, and family. In this way, overidentification with a persona restricts emotional intimacy and personal growth.

EXERCISE: CREATING A PERSONA MASK

Think about the card you most identify with in the tarot. Many of us have that one tarot card we gravitate toward that we feel represents who we are as a person. This card could be a representation of your persona. Find this card in the deck and set it aside.

We are going to create a persona-inspired mask with tarot as our guide. Using a blank sheet of paper, start doodling, drawing, or writing to represent ways the tarot archetype you chose represents your persona. Use colors, symbols, or words that capture the essence of the persona you present to the world. This side of the paper represents how you wish to be seen—your external identity, aspirations, and social persona.

Next, flip your mask over. Now, reflect on the emotions, fears, and thoughts that this persona (or mask) helps you to conceal from others.

What do you hide behind the mask that you present to the world? You can use drawings, words, or symbols to express these hidden aspects. If you want to continue incorporating tarot, you could shuffle and pull a few cards to help guide you. Or you could intentionally go through your deck stopping at the cards that elicit an emotional response. Use these images and archetypes to help fill in the inside of your mask. This side represents your internal experience—the qualities that may not align with societal expectations or your persona.

Once you have created both sides of your mask, take some time to consider the contrast between them.

⇒ *Reflect* ⇐

What feelings come up for you when you observe both sides of your mask?

_____

_____

_____

_____

_____

Are there aspects of your hidden self that you wish to integrate into your public persona?

_____

_____

_____

_____

_____

How might overidentifying with your persona limit your emotional expression and connections with others?

_____

_____

_____

_____

FUNCTIONS OF THE SHADOW

Even when we try to ignore our shadow, the shadow still exists. Denying the shadow and pushing it away can cause it to emerge more intensely and become more persistent. It can often emerge in the form of projection, where we accuse or blame other people for behaving in ways that we are actually struggling with ourselves. This can negatively impact our relationships, shape how we see and experience the world, and muddy our own understanding of ourself.

Complexes as a Function of the Shadow

A complex is an organized group of thoughts, emotions, memories, and perceptions that are often unconscious but strongly influence an individual's behavior and self-perception. Complexes are often the result of unprocessed trauma, tension, or conflict, and they have significant, unconscious influence on our thoughts, feelings, and actions. A complex can form or strengthen when our shadows interact with an issue we are struggling with. The shadow and the complex work together in that the shadow provides the material to create a complex, and then the complex reinforces the material of the shadow by acting out or behaving in a way that keeps our shadow hidden and repressed.

Complexes are powerful in that they function autonomously and can distort our perception of reality and create deeply rooted narratives about ourselves and the world around us. Jung viewed the ego as the core, dominant complex that gives us a stable sense of identity—what we know to be true about ourselves. However, he also believed there are many other selves or parts within us. While these parts don't seek the same level of stability and control as the ego, each part has the ability to influence the way we think and behave.

Complexes, though they can lead to discomfort and pain, are not necessarily something we need to be working to "heal" or get rid of, just like we don't need to erase, or "heal," our shadows. However, we do need to be working to discover these parts of ourselves so we can function fully and not just exist from the perspective of a complex or shadow.

For example, an inferiority complex (feeling as though we are not good enough) could form in childhood when someone experiences repeated belittlement and criticism while vulnerably sharing their true Self, or if they are unfavorably compared to others in ways that make them feel unimportant, or "less than." In this case, the shadow would be linked to a trait that was belittled, and the complex would be the personal narrative of feeling worthless or feeling that they should hide their true Self. Over time, this inferiority complex might dominate a person's actions, leading them to overcompensate (constantly working to prove their worth) or retreat from situations that trigger feelings of inadequacy (avoid taking risks because they feel like they will just fail anyway).

We can explore this complex further through the tarot archetype of the Star. As a shadow, the Star represents the repression of vulnerability and avoidance of authenticity. While traditionally the Star symbolizes healing, openness, and renewal, its shadow reflects the fear of being seen. This repression might develop from past experiences where vulnerability was met with rejection or criticism as mentioned earlier. In this case, someone who previously would have been comfortable performing in front of a crowd, sharing their inner thoughts and feelings, or working on projects that lead to recognition from others, now has a shadow around this level of vulnerability and might find themselves annoyed or jealous of folks who express themselves in those ways.

In an attempt to protect the Self, a person might suppress their true emotions, choose to wear a mask of stoicism, or resort to measures of conformity to avoid further emotional pain. In this shadowed state, the Star's capacity for healing and growth becomes obscured by layers of fear and self-doubt. This repression of authenticity can also arise from a belief that the true Self is inadequate or unworthy. This leads to behaviors where the individual presents a watered-down version of themselves, disconnecting from their raw emotional state in order to avoid being vulnerable or truly seen by others.

We can then explore the Six of Pentacles as a possible complex born from the shadow of the Star. This archetype is often associated with giving and receiving, generosity, and a sense of personal and communal balance.

When viewed through the lens of the Star's shadow, the Six of Pentacles reveals a distortion in how we view our worthiness, especially in relation to others.

For example, the fear of vulnerability associated with the shadow of the Star may lead individuals to overcompensate by giving excessively to others as a way to prove their value (Six of Pentacles). This could manifest as overextending oneself, offering more than they are comfortable with, or attempting to earn love through material or emotional generosity. This is similar to codependency or people pleasing. Conversely, some may reject receiving affection or help from others because their shadow and complex have left them feeling unworthy of love or fearing the emotional exposure that comes with accepting it. This complex often results in an unbalanced dynamic where the individual continually gives but struggles to express their own needs, leading to emotional exhaustion and resentment.

For someone carrying the shadow of the Star and a complex rooted in the Six of Pentacles, they might judge or criticize individuals who openly express vulnerability or emotional needs as a form of projection. This type of projection could be explored through the archetype of the King of Cups. This archetype could represent a projection of envy or disdain toward those who embrace authentic, emotional vulnerability. Because the person struggling with their own repressed vulnerability feels inadequate, they might label others as "needy" or "entitled" when, in reality, these judgments are reflections of their own unacknowledged desires for emotional expression.

Projections as a Function of the Shadow

> Projection is an unconscious mechanism that is employed whenever
> a trait or characteristic of our personality that has no relationship
> to consciousness becomes activated.

—WILLIAM A. MILLER

Projection, again, is a common form of reactivity from the repressed shadow, where we assign our own undesirable qualities or emotions onto someone else in an attempt to further distance ourselves from our own shadow. The shadow self feels uncomfortable, anxious, and irritated when confronted with certain situations or people who trigger these hidden parts. Recognizing these signs of projection is often the first step toward understanding and integrating the shadow into our conscious awareness. When we ignore them, we create a container of unexamined parts that end up having a significant influence on the way we function.

During my graduate studies, I undertook an internship at a domestic violence shelter under the supervision of a Licensed Clinical Social Worker. Our supervision sessions, which involved staffing cases and coordinating client care, frequently evolved into impromptu lessons on trauma and self-awareness. I vividly recall one session where my supervisor explained the concept of being triggered, although she referred to it as being "hooked." She sketched a peanut-shaped figure on a piece of paper, filling it with numerous "x" shapes, then drew another similarly marked peanut figure. She described these figures as people, with the "x" shapes representing feelings, experiences, and traumas. She explained that when we interact with others, we metaphorically cast out an invisible fishing line with a hook. Occasionally, this hook catches onto something within us, triggering a reaction. That hook can sting! This reaction can then manifest as a projection, as the interaction or experience with another person hooks onto a corresponding trait within us. In essence, projecting a shadow onto someone else stops us from taking responsibility or ownership of this shadow.

Jungian analyst William A. Miller uses similar language to describe projection encounters with the shadow by explaining how others must have "hooks" that our projections can attach to. Remember, projection is not a conscious act; it serves as a form of self-preservation and a means to avoid confronting aspects of ourselves or our shadow. However, just because projections happen unconsciously, that doesn't mean we can avoid accountability. It is still our responsibility to recognize them and stay aware of when they show up.

Tarot is a beneficial tool for exploring the shadow and its functions because it provides a visual outlet to witness shadow material and its complexes and projections in a safe and accessible way. Throughout my time as a tarot practitioner, I have observed that certain cards, such as the Emperor and the Hierophant, are almost universally disliked. Since the shadow represents behaviors or feelings within us that we don't want to acknowledge but can easily identify in others, looking at cards we dislike might help to uncover a personal shadow. The Emperor, for instance, traditionally symbolizes power, control, and authority. Individuals who struggle with this card often express disdain for those who seek to control, exert power over others, and enjoy authoritarian roles. While mild reactions to these traits are common, a vehement dislike for this card may indicate a shadow. If this sounds like you, sit with that card for a moment. When do you seek control? When do you try to exert power? In what ways do you enjoy roles of authority?

In *Meeting the Shadow*, philosopher Ken Wilber says, "If a person or thing in the environment informs us, we probably aren't projecting. On the other hand, if it affects us, chances are that we are victims of our own projections."

We can look at this through the lens of tarot archetypes. Applying the concept of projection to the Emperor suggests that individuals affected by this archetype and who express strong feelings toward this card may possess similar traits of seeking power and control. Since these traits are part of their shadow, these individuals could be distancing themselves from them by way of projection: expressions of disgust, verbal criticism, scoffing, eye-rolling, or labeling the card as "bad." However, these reactions only deepen the shadow.

The healthier, integrated reaction is to recognize these projections and use them as opportunities for self-discovery rather than becoming ensnared in a cycle of judgment and avoidance. With the Emperor, it can feel terrifying to acknowledge that you might be someone capable of engaging in controlling behavior because it has been labeled as a "bad" or even "abusive" trait. It's not inherently "bad" or "wrong" to have controlling traits or to enjoy being in positions of authority. How you handle yourself when you are in control or have power is what matters. Are you being harmful or helpful? Are you leading or forcing? There is a big difference.

⇒ *Reflect* ⇐

What traits do you dislike in others?

_____

_____

_____

_____

_____

Rate the intensity of your dislike for each trait on a scale from 1 to 10 (1 = mild dislike, 10 = intense dislike).

_____

_____

_____

_____

_____

How would your life or relationships be different if these reactions "informed" you instead of "affected" you?

_____

_____

_____

_____

_____

Exercise: Shadow Timeline

Timelines can be powerful tools to identify shadows, complexes, and projections. In psychotherapy, I often use timelines to better understand my clients and help guide them to better understand and process specific events in their life. While this exercise can be fun and enlightening, it can also bring up memories that are painful or that you are not yet prepared to process. Please listen to your body and only do as much as you feel comfortable doing.

You are invited to utilize this version of the timeline technique through the use of tarot and other magickal tools that are prominent in your practice such as stones, incense, or pendulums. You may want to include stones that are reminiscent of different times in your life or that represent what you need most as you work through this exercise. For example, you may choose to use hematite at your altar to feel safe and reduce anxiety. Or perhaps you find clear quartz useful for clarity and amethyst helpful for spiritual focus and support. As you prepare to work through this exercise, you might choose to bring in additional elements for soothing support (e.g., incense for cleansing and calming properties).

This exercise can be completed in several formats. One way to complete it is by laying your cards out face up and choosing the cards that represent specific moments throughout your life (e.g., early childhood, adolescence, early adult, middle adult, etc.). You may choose to pull up to ten cards after shuffling and analyze each card to see where on your personal timeline they fit best. Or you may choose to use your pendulum to help guide you toward the cards most needed for this exercise.

Choose, pull, or allow your pendulum to guide you toward the cards to represent your life timeline starting with early childhood, moving toward adolescence, early adulthood, up until wherever you are currently. You may choose one, two, or three cards to represent each phase of your life.

Once you have selected your cards, use the reflection questions below to help guide you through processing your timeline.

- In what ways have these experiences shaped you?

- What messages about yourself were formed during this time?

- What narrative did you develop about others during this time?

- Where does your shadow emerge in these experiences?

- What complexes are present?

- How can you reclaim times you felt powerless?

- What does your present Self want to say to your past Self?

After you have completed your life timeline, shuffle the remaining cards and separate the deck into three piles. Flip each pile over. The bottom card of each pile represents the following completion to each phrase below:

- I forgive myself for ...

- I currently need ...

- I am working toward ...

Shadow Timeline: Client Example

I once used this exercise with a client who was feeling stuck. They were having a difficult time accessing memories from certain parts of their life and making connections as to why they were feeling the way they did at present. In this example, I will explain just the first portion of their timeline and their reflections.

The three cards that they chose to represent their early childhood were the Empress (reversed), Six of Swords, and the Hanged One. The client realized through the Empress reversed that they never received the caring, compassionate, and nurturing love from their mother that they truly needed. Often, their mother would dismiss their needs by telling them to take care of things themselves (Six of Swords), and the client often felt the need to be alone with or ignore their feelings because they were deemed unimportant.

The client realized the emergence of a shadow during this exercise that was directly related to their experience with the Empress and the Six of Swords. They acknowledged they became annoyed and agitated when they saw people asking for help, care, or comfort. The client felt it was "needy" and showed a lack of independence. This shadow was directly linked to the client's "mother" complex.

In this exercise, they felt that the Hanged One showed how confused they were as a child and how disorienting it was to process difficult emotions and struggles on their own. This led to them pulling the Five of Pentacles for the prompt "I forgive myself for . . . ," which they promptly acknowledged as needing to forgive themselves for denying help and care from others. Growing up they were made to feel like a burden, and the pain of feeling burdensome was stronger than the pain someone else might help alleviate for them.

THE PROCESS OF INDIVIDUATION

The goal of shadow work is individuation and integration. We will explore the concept of shadow integration in Chapter 7. In therapy, individuation refers to the process of becoming one's most authentic Self by integrating all aspects of the personality, both conscious and unconscious. Through individuation, we become more self-aware, less governed by unconscious forces, and better able to balance all parts of our psyche. This journey is not about achieving perfection but about embracing complexity and duality. Jung saw individuation as a necessary path of psychological development, in which the ego gains awareness of its own inner substance and life's greater meaning. Essentially, Jung believed that individuation leads to feelings of wholeness. For therapists, guiding clients through individuation often brings them to a place of increased self-compassion—a place we all deserve to reach.

This process also involves integrating conflicting aspects of the Self in order to experience internal harmony, which is precisely what shadow work allows us to do. In Dialectical Behavior Therapy (DBT), one of the core principles is that two opposing ideas can exist at the same time. Therapists often use the phrase "Two things can be true," when explaining this concept. This is important to keep in mind when navigating our shadow world because we can possess qualities we admire alongside traits we dislike. Acknowledging and embracing this tension is a significant marker of individuation and shadow assimilation.

A pivotal part of individuation is confronting the parts of ourselves we have hidden or denied (much like shadow work). As we work toward accepting these parts, we become more whole, integrated, and authentic. We can liken it to piecing together a puzzle: once the puzzle is complete, we can see the full image clearly. The puzzle's ridges and lines, representing our experiences and moments of growth, remain visible, indicating that the process isn't seamless, nor should it be. Many people imagine individuation as a final stop on the journey of self-actualization, but it's not. The truth is, we are never truly done.

Think about the Fool's journey through the lens of tarot. The Fool's journey is a symbolic narrative reflecting the stages and experiences of life, a process of self-discovery, growth, and transformation. The Fool begins their adventure with naivety, carrying a small bag representing potential and lessons yet to be learned, as well as their shadows. Each new experience means beginning again as the Fool. In fact, we often undergo multiple Fool's journeys simultaneously, much like individuation—a constant journey toward wholeness and self-realization.

The process of integrating aspects of the unconscious and conscious mind is about reconciling our inner conflicts to achieve greater balance and completeness. Each tarot card can represent an aspect of individuation and shadow work, but the archetype of the World stands out as a symbol of completion, fulfillment, and integration. It embodies the essence of individuation and the shadow work journey. However, we are never truly finished with this process. Reaching a sense of wholeness regarding one aspect of our shadow simply makes space for the next leg of the journey to begin. To be alive is to continually be experiencing this cycle.

The Fool's journey and individuation are both daunting yet rewarding adventures. Having shadow parts and working to acknowledge and integrate them doesn't mean something is wrong with us. It doesn't make us "bad" or broken—it means we are human. The imagery of the World archetype from the traditional Rider-Waite-Smith tarot reflects this. In the card, a figure is encircled by a wreath, symbolizing cyclical renewal and regeneration. The elements of earth, air, fire, and water surrounding the figure signify the harmonious alignment of conscious and unconscious forces—a state of equilibrium that individuation and shadow work strive to achieve.

The figure in the World represents wholeness and unity, reflecting the integration of contrasting aspects of the Self. The wreath's circular shape evokes the ongoing, cyclical process of growth and transformation in both individuation and shadow work. This continuum reminds us that the journey of self-discovery is lifelong.

Remember that the Self refers to our core, authentic essence—the compassionate, curious, and wise part that exists within each of us, which mimics the Self we explored through the lens of Internal Family Systems (IFS) work. This core Self is where true healing and integration unfold within our inner system. The World card aligns well with this idea, serving as an anchor for both shadow work and the journey of individuation. As you continue to move through your shadow work journey, consider using the World card as a visual reminder of the authentic, unburdened Self you are uncovering and working toward embodying. It represents the goal of integration, wholeness, and continuous growth.

EXERCISE: WORKING WITH THE ARCHETYPE OF THE WORLD

Grab a tarot deck and find the World card. Pay attention to the artwork and the details. Think about what the card and its symbols could represent when you think of individuation. Now reflect on what it would mean to feel more whole or integrated, as if you were embodying the energy of the World card.

Reflect

What would be different about how you treat yourself if you were working towards wholeness?

_____

_____

_____

_____

_____

How would you show up differently in your relationships with others?

_____

_____

_____

_____

_____

In what ways do you see your own core Self represented in the World card?

_____

_____

_____

_____

_____

Chapter 4

The Psychology of Magick and Shadow Work

Everything that works magically is incomprehensible, and the incomprehensible often works magically.

—CARL JUNG

WHAT IS MAGICK?

While my approach to shadow work is deeply rooted in secular, therapeutic, and psychological principles, I recognize the valuable role that magick, archetypes, and symbolism play in this process. Tarot, for instance, serves as a potent tool for self-reflection, offering a portal to our subconscious and helping us access parts of ourselves that we otherwise may have been unable to access. The imagery and archetypes can also help facilitate a dialogue with our shadow, making it easier to converse with the repressed and hidden parts of ourselves.

Magick, the occult, and occult tools (such as tarot) are a way to enhance our intuition, improve our relationships with ourselves and others, and bring our subconscious to the surface in order to feel increased awareness, curiosity, and contentment. To be drawn to magick and mysticism means we are inherently drawn to the shadow, to the unknown, and to depth.

Magickal tools like tarot can easily catapult us into a world where anything seems possible and accessible because the magick of tarot is not just in its visual appeal, but in the stories the cards are able to tell us, and the stories the cards allow us to tell. Along with all of that possibility, magickal tools give us opportunities to discover the shadow parts of us that may have otherwise remained hidden.

I think it is important to remind ourselves that the magick of tarot resides within each of us—the interpreters, or readers, of the cards, and not necessarily the cards themselves. It is our intuition, our understanding, and our connection and relationship to the symbols, the stories, and the archetypes that give the cards meaning and ultimately the magickal experience we are seeking. This is why, even though the cards all have their own traditional meanings, they can still be understood and experienced in an infinite number of ways. Each person reading the cards is infusing, or projecting, a part of themselves into the interpretation and the story the card is telling and the story they are telling about the card. This process, I think, is the true magick of tarot.

My professional work these days seems to be planted firmly at the intersection of logic and magick. Here I am, a staunch proponent for evidenced-based practices, yet I loudly advocate for tools like tarot to be normalized for self-reflection and healing. To create harmony and reduce tension between the logical and mystical aspects of ourselves, we need to be curious about multiple ways of being, experiment with how these ways of being impact us (for better or for worse), and then figure out what to do with this information.

To embrace our logical side is to understand the psychological mechanisms behind magickal tools like tarot and appreciate it as a mechanism for personal growth and introspection. When we work to embrace these tools, we inevitably recognize that they are simply a conduit for our own inner wisdom. In doing so, we are able to become better acquainted with all of our various parts, personal narratives, and shadows. On the other hand, embracing our mystical side invites us to step into a place of playful curiosity and creativity, which encourages us to honor the inherent beauty of the unknown, as well as any spiritual or magickal connection that tarot and other tools might be able to offer. It encourages us to trust in our intuition and the idea that there is always more to life than what we experience at the conscious level.

Magick, in this context, becomes a lens through which we can view the world. Magick can function as an invitation to explore the hidden, shadowy areas of our own consciousness and work with it. It's like having multiple pairs of glasses to wear based on our mood or outfit that day. How are you feeling? Do you want to wear your logical lenses or your magickal lenses? Perhaps it's worth trying on both so you can check out the view through each before you decide. To maintain a clear mind for decision-making and feel fully integrated and balanced, we need to practice navigating between these two worlds.

The metaphorical lenses I am talking about show us different mental and emotional terrain, so we need to alternate between them to make sure we are navigating the world around us with balance and ease. In doing so, we can truly harness the whole power of tarot, and other magickal tools. If we are only ever wearing our analytical and logical lenses and we neglect the magickal lenses, we could be robbing ourselves of opportunities to discover new truths about ourself.

Jung approached magick and the occult with both an analytical and mystical mind. He considered occult practices as a valuable field for exploring the depths of the human psyche as well as the connection between our internal and external world. Jung's theories highlighted the value of myth, symbolism, and ritual (often central to occult practices) in helping us understand the collective unconscious. Jung went so far as to acknowledge the importance of alchemy, describing the process of alchemical transformation as mirroring the process of individuation.

Ultimately, I believe magick is the human experience we have each day. It is everything we embody, it's the choices we make, the art we create, and the relationships we build. Magick is our ability to think, feel, do, and dream.

MALADAPTIVE MAGICK

It's worth noting the distinction I make between "magical" and "magickal" throughout this book and specifically this section. The spelling of "magick" with a *k* is often used in spiritual and occult communities to differentiate between stage, or entertainment, "magic" with a c (like illusions). Magick with a *k* is fueled by intention, autonomy, and free will.

When I refer to magickal thinking with a *k*, I'm speaking to the symbolic, archetypal, and ritualistic use of tools like tarot to engage with, and explore, the unconscious. In this case, it's not a form of entertainment (or even witchcraft in the traditional sense), but a psychological and therapeutic lens through which we can gain a clearer view of ourselves and our potential.

Now, to throw another definition of magic with a *c* into the mix, we need to consider the psychological concept of magical thinking. In the field of psychology, magical thinking is a belief that one's ideas, thoughts, actions, or words can influence events in the material world, often without a plausible causal link. For example, a tarot reader may believe that only cards that jump out during shuffling are valid because they're guided by spirit and should be given more weight, or read over cards that don't jump out. This is not inherently maladaptive. It only becomes maladaptive if this belief leads to excessive shuffling and a disruption of daily activities, or begins to cause discomfort. Similarly, the belief that drinking a specific tea will bring good fortune can be a healthy form of magical thinking, but if this belief escalates to the point where the individual attributes all positive or negative events to whether or not they drank that specific tea, then it becomes a cognitive distortion and therefore maladaptive magical thinking.

Maladaptive magical thinking extends beyond simple superstitions and steps into rigid, pervasive beliefs and cognitive distortions that impair an individual's ability to fully function. For instance, consider the cognitive distortion where a single negative event, such as spilling your morning coffee, is perceived as a precursor to a terrible day (we've all been there). This thought pattern triggers a cognitive bias, leading the individual to overly focus on subsequent negative events while ignoring any positive ones, which then creates a cycle where the initial belief (that spilling the coffee meant the day was going to be terrible) is reinforced. Maladaptive magick can also exist when we struggle to distinguish our magickal practices and tools from our own personal autonomy. In my role as a psychotherapist, tools such as tarot, crystals, and incense serve as complementary aids that are most beneficial when integrated with evidence-based practices and not as a predictive, divinatory function.

As a secular practitioner, I find my interactions with the cards function primarily as a cognitive, or thought, exercise. In my experience, the cards themselves do not perform the work and are not magic. Instead, they allow me to tap into different areas of consciousness that can offer guidance and reveal specific thoughts, memories, ideas, or emotions, which can make the experience feel magickal. This distinction is important so as not to solely rely on magickal tools like tarot for self-exploration, healing, or answers to your questions. The cards are not prescriptive—they should not be dictating actions, feelings, or thoughts. Instead, they are most helpful when acting as a bridge, that allows us to access hidden parts of ourself.

EXERCISE: BALANCING THE TENSION BETWEEN LOGIC AND MAGICK

Grab a tarot deck. Shuffle, then pull three cards.

Card 1: A representation of your relationship to magick

Card 2: A representation of your relationship to logic

Card 3: Guidance on how to manage the tension between logic and magick

⤜ *Reflect* ⤛

My cards for this exercise are:

Card 1: _____

Thoughts: _____

_____

_____

_____

_____

Card 2: _____

Thoughts: _____

_____

_____

_____

_____

Card 3: _____

Thoughts: _____

_____

_____

_____

_____

MAGICKAL TOOLS FOR SHADOW WORK

Before my therapy practice went completely virtual, I had the office of my dreams. It was a large, four-office suite with a lobby, kitchenette, and bathroom. I had an end unit, so there were floor-to-ceiling windows from the lobby all the way down one whole side of the building. The windows looked out to a lush courtyard with 100-year-old oak trees, wild snake plants, and blooming birds of paradise. It was magickal. Inside my office was no different. I always wanted my clients to feel like they were stepping into a calm, safe space. I wanted their nervous systems to regulate just by walking through the front door. So I had lots of warm lighting, relaxing music, water features, salt rock lamps, and plenty of crystals. I have always loved crystals, but I never realized how surprisingly important they would become to my therapy practice.

In the room where I saw clients, there were two side tables and a bookshelf that held a collection of my favorite therapy books along with a plethora of crystals, stones, and other objects for folks to fidget with if they needed to. I made it a point to tell each client that they were welcome to grab anything in my office they felt drawn to or needed to hold at any point during our work together.

I kept a clear quartz point on a side table along with a few tumbled stones like amethyst, sodalite, rose quartz, and aventurine. Without fail, everyone gravitated toward the clear crystal point. Clients would even grab it as soon as they walked into the office, letting it balance between their fingers or turn it around in their hands, staring at it deeply as they shared their stories with me. Often, I would gravitate toward it too.

In between clients, I would find myself needing to ground and regulate my own nervous system. I had a few different interventions I would cycle through: lavender and sage room spray, diaphragmatic breathing, a few minutes of a yoga pose, a walk around the block, or a few stretches. However, more often than not, I was reaching for that clear quartz point. I loved how cold it felt in my hands. I would often hold it against my chest while I took several deep breaths if I was having a particularly emotional day. There was something so special about this stone.

Fast-forward a few years and my practice is now completely virtual. I, of course, kept the majority of my office decor—especially my stones. I keep them on my desk now so I can see them during sessions. I don't reach for them as often as I used to, but when I need them, they are there. In fact, recently, during my own personal therapy that clear crystal point became the central focus.

My schedule was slammed, so I had to switch my appointment with my own therapist to a virtual session at the last minute. I had a lot of significant life changes happening at the time, and I knew there would be a lot of crying during this session. Not even five minutes into the appointment and I already had a fistful of tissues at the ready. My therapist is rooted in somatic-based practices, so she immediately helped me ground and regulate my nervous system. First she asked me to look around the room and locate an object that might calm me. I immediately spotted the clear quartz point.

As I held the quartz and rolled it between my fingers, my therapist immediately noticed my breathing had slowed down. She asked me what was happening for me at that moment. I recalled the times my clients held this same crystal in their hands, noticing its cool temperature, zooming in on the imperfections in the stone, and running their fingertips over the pointed edge. My eyes welled up again, but this time with gratitude and love for the clients who allowed me to hold space for them when they were in the same type of moment I was in now, with my own therapist. Before I knew it, ten minutes of me staring into this stone had gone by. My breathing was now slow and steady. My thoughts were clearer, and I was ready and able to talk about what was going on. I eventually set the stone down but kept it in front of me for the remainder of the session.

Not only can the use of crystals and stones act as a calming tool during the shadow work process, but they can also provide additional insight into the work you are doing. Paying attention to the types of stones and magickal tools you are gravitating toward can help paint a picture of what is happening in the subconscious.

RITUAL AS A MAGICKAL TOOL

In rituals, the most ordinary of actions and gestures become transformed into symbolic expressions, their meaning reinforced each time they are performed.
—ARNOLD VAN GENNEP

Rituals have long been known to provide a structured space to engage with our beliefs, needs, wants, and desires. Designing a personal ritual for our shadow work journey allows us to create a safe space to explore and integrate the parts of ourselves we have hidden or rejected. By creating a sacred container for shadow work, we can infuse this practice with safety, compassion, and intentionality.

A ritual is a frequently performed action that holds symbolic significance and helps us establish a sense of continuity and stability in our everyday lives. Rituals are structured, deliberate actions that are performed with intention. Contrary to how we often view rituals, they are not solely cultural or religious practices; a ritual is also a psychological tool that can greatly impact our mental and emotional well-being.

Once you start to understand and absorb the concept of shadow work, you will find that you are doing this work all the time—at work, in the car, while grocery shopping, at dinners with friends, etc. Because the shadow can emerge in our normal daily life, there will not always be an opportunity to engage in a formal ritual to signify the beginning of your shadow work exercise or the end of it. So we will explore ways you can create multiple rituals depending on where you are, what you are doing, and the level of accessibility you need.

In Chapter 1, we explored the idea of creating a shadow work altar. This would be an ideal space to engage in a deeper type of shadow work ritual if you are intentionally stepping into the world of the shadow for focused work. A ritual at your altar might include lighting specific incense, grounding with a crystal or stone, or reciting a mantra while engaging in a diaphragmatic breathing exercise. This is the typical formula we think of when we think of ritual. However, simply stepping into a room, turning on a specific lamp, and sitting down the same way can be a ritual. We don't always have to be fancy or ornate when it comes to rituals.

From a psychological perspective, engaging in a ritual as part of your shadow work journey can also help regulate intense emotions. In a 2018 review of research, "The Psychology of Rituals: An Integrative Review and Process-Based Framework" found that rituals act as a means of shielding us against the detrimental consequences of intense or negative emotions. In fact, we are naturally more inclined to engage in ritual-like behaviors under conditions marked by negative emotions, including stress, anxiety, and uncertainty. It is like our bodies know we need to self-soothe and regulate.

Example of a Shadow Work Ritual

When designing a formal shadow work ritual, you may choose to incorporate candle magick. If this aligns with your journey, researching the meanings of candle colors can help personalize your ritual and tailor it to your own needs. For example, you may choose to light a black candle for protection and a blue candle for emotional healing at the start of your shadow work ritual.

As you plan and design your ritual, think about additional items that symbolize protection and guidance. This might include crystals such as clear quartz for promoting a sense of emotional balance and amethyst for easing anxiety. Perhaps you have a smooth, tumbled stone you like to hold in your hand as you step into the world of your shadow because it helps keep you present and grounded. Or maybe you like to have a specific song or music genre playing in the background. These objects serve as anchors, reminding you of your intention and providing comfort.

Mantras or intentional phrases can also be beneficial additions to a ritual. In fact, mantras have been shown to help reduce anxiety and stress. So creating a mantra or phrase that highlights patience, self-compassion, and radical acceptance can help set the tone for an emotionally regulated shadow work experience. Exploring the shadow can be intense and stir up intense and confusing thoughts about ourselves, so having a phrase or mantra accessible can help us balance any emotional intensity that may arise.

Stepping out of shadow work is equally as important as stepping into it. Designing a ritual for stepping out of shadow work helps to close the process and gently reintegrate you back into your daily life. To conclude, you might consider expressing gratitude for the insights and experiences gained, repeat the phrase or mantra that you opened with, or recite a specific closing mantra.

Phrases or mantras you might want to include as you step into a shadow work practice include:

- "I am patient with my journey, compassionate with my struggles, and accepting of my true self."

- "I embrace my shadows with kindness, patience, and curiosity."

- "I welcome every part of myself."

- "I am learning and growing at my own pace."

- "I am worthy of my own compassion."

Reflect

I encourage you to reflect on what might feel natural to say to yourself in these moments. Perhaps it is a combination of any of the suggestions above, or maybe you have created your own phrase or mantra. Use the space below to brainstorm personal mantras for your personal practice.

_____

_____

_____

_____

_____

_____

_____

_____

_____

_____

_____

_____

_____

_____

_____

SIGILS AND THE SHADOW

Another way to incorporate magickal practices into shadow work is through the creation and use of sigils. The process of creating a sigil in the context of shadow work allows us to move from an abstract thought or experience that we might feel disconnected from to create a tangible symbol that bypasses the critical, rational mind in order to access deeper levels of consciousness.

A sigil is a visual symbol that holds purpose and intention. When we create a sigil, we are putting our thoughts, ideas, desires, etc., into a tangible form that becomes embedded in our subconscious, making us more likely to embody what the sigil means to us. This is similar to the concept of manifestation. With manifestation, we take time to write down our dreams, goals, and desires. In doing so, we are more likely to achieve or "manifest" them. Research backs this up. Sigils just take this process further through the creative component of symbolism.

Austin Osman Spare is well known for creating the sigil manifestation method. His creation and use of sigils was his primary method of accessing the unconscious. Spare's approach to creating sigils involved condensing a written desire into a more streamlined form. He would eliminate any repeated letters from the statement (folks will often remove vowels as well), and then merge the remaining characters into a unique symbol. Spare believed this symbol was meant to be embedded in the mind and then consciously forgotten.

The process of creating sigils operates on the subconscious level, which responds more naturally to symbols than to language, allowing the sigil to work in the background to help manifest the intended outcome. This concept can also be applied to the use of mantras during shadow work. Reflecting on the mantras introduced earlier in the chapter, transforming one into a sigil offers the subconscious a powerful tool to engage with throughout the shadow work journey. This practice can support nervous system regulation and provide comfort when confronting difficult truths.

Just like writing down a goal makes it more likely to happen, turning your intention into a sigil helps your mind take it more seriously. Letting yourself forget about the sigil afterward is like setting an intention and then letting go of the need to control the outcome and trusting that your subconscious will keep working on it in the background. In this way, the sigil becomes an active tool for both self-reflection and transformation, aligning with the larger goal of shadow work: integrating hidden aspects of the Self to promote personal growth.

Example of a Sigil

Let's take the mantra "I am worthy of my own compassion." Using Austin Osman Spare's method, we'll start by removing all vowels and any repeating letters from this statement. What remains are the letters F, M, W, R, T, H, Y, N, C, P, S. These remaining letters are the building blocks of your sigil. From here, you can get creative by combining and arranging these letters into a unique symbol that holds the energy of your intention.

Use the space below to create your own sigil to accompany you on your shadow work journey.

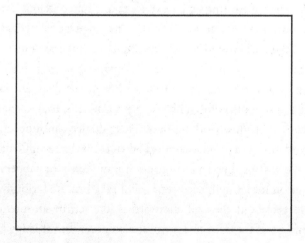

MAGICKAL PRACTICES AS A FORM OF PSYCHODRAMA

As someone who sits at the intersection of magick and logic, I often compare the practice of magick and shadow work to psychodrama. Psychodrama was created by psychiatrist Dr. Jacob Levy Moreno and later expanded upon in collaboration with his wife, psychotherapist Zerka Moreno. Moreno introduced psychodrama in the early twentieth century as a method involving role-playing and improvisation to assist patients in exploring their emotions and experiences. He argued that traditional talk therapy was restrictive, because he saw it as only encouraging patients to *discuss* their feelings rather than actively *express* and process them.

Psychodrama, on the other hand, allows patients to act out their thoughts, feelings, and experiences in a safe, controlled environment that advocates for creativity. In this way, psychodrama provides a more tangible means for patients to gain insight into their emotions and experiences. This experiential approach allows us to fully embody our thoughts and feelings and safely experiment with new ways of being.

Essentially, Moreno created psychodrama to encourage patients to leverage their inherent creativity in order to authentically express themselves with the goal of being able to acknowledge new ways of thinking and being. I have found that the concept of magick, and more specifically the use of tarot, operates in much the same way, making them beneficial psychodrama companions.

In the therapy room, psychodrama can take on many creative forms. Often, role-playing is utilized to help clients explore, act, or reenact difficult relationship experiences or unresolved emotional issues in a safe, controlled space. In these sessions, clients act out scenes from their lives as if they were characters in a play or movie, allowing them to embody and externalize their emotions in ways that traditional talk therapy would not allow. By externalizing their inner world and bringing their "scenes" to life, sometimes in overly dramatized ways, clients are able to experience deeper levels of healing and understanding.

When we perform a ritual, practice magick, or pull tarot cards, we are, in essence, acting out a psychodrama. We are taking something intangible and making it tangible. We are creating a space where we give our internal world permission to exist outside of us—if even for just a brief moment. For example, an altar or ritual becomes a miniature stage where we are able to explore and act out some of our deepest fears and innermost desires. This metaphorical stage that ritual has created gives us permission to explore aspects of ourselves that otherwise would have remained hidden in the unconscious. Through the psychodrama of magick, we can better understand our internal, unconscious world and perhaps work on transforming it in the process.

We could look at the ritual of cord cutting as a form of psychodrama: lighting two candles bound by string to sever a connection or unwanted attachment. The candles, string, flame, and the act of lighting it are all physical representations of our intent. Through this ritual, we are not *only* symbolically cutting ties with someone or something; we are enacting a psychodrama where we confront and conquer our fears and desires in the process.

Another example is the art of manifestation, specifically through writing. When we write down a goal, we are not merely jotting down a wish. We are performing a ritual, an act imbued with intent. This process mirrors the principles of magick and psychodrama where our internal world is explored externally with the goal of creating a specific outcome.

In this case, through the lens of magickal psychodrama, the pen could represent a talisman and the written word a spell. Or a tarot card is the talisman and the interpretation or reflection is a spell. Together, they create a tangible representation of our inner world. In psychodrama, the act of reenacting experiences allows us to step into a different role, to view our challenges and desires from a new perspective. Writing down our goals and desires works in much the same way. It allows us to externalize our intentions, to see them laid out before us, and to interact with them in a more physical and immediate manner. This act of externalization helps clarify our objectives and solidifies our commitment to them.

In fact, research supports this theory of manifestation. One 2015 study conducted at Dominican University found that we are 33 percent more likely to achieve our goals if we physically write them down. Another study published in the *Journal of Applied Psychology* called "The Effect of Goal Setting on Group Performance" found that we are 42 percent more likely to achieve our goals when we write them down. If we apply these same theories and research to shadow work, the psychodrama component inherent within this work is likely to increase our chances of experiencing the outcome we desire from our shadow work journey.

Essentially, the psychodrama of shadow work as a magickal practice can be seen as a profound psychological tool. It provides a structured way to confront the tension within us and bring us closer to feeling inner balance and clarity. Just as psychodrama allows us to rehearse real-life scenarios and emotions in a controlled environment, magick as a psychodrama permits us to experiment with and manipulate the forces at play in our lives.

By engaging with these practices, we create a dialogue between the conscious and the unconscious, the seen and the unseen. It's a way to make the invisible visible, to give shape to the shapeless. In this way, magick is a form of self-therapy, a method to explore the depths of our psyche and emerge with a greater understanding of ourselves and the world around us.

Engaging with the Shadow through Psychodrama

Early in my career, my training focused on working with families, particularly those experiencing high levels of conflict and trauma. Traditional talk therapy proved less effective in these situations, prompting us to adopt a variety of experiential techniques. We frequently employed modalities such as psychodrama, play therapy, sand-tray therapy, art therapy, and other hands-on approaches to facilitate connection among family members, regulate their nervous systems, and explore new methods of communication, understanding, and healing.

One exercise that particularly resonated with me involved the use of objects and symbols to represent individuals and experiences pertinent to the family members' current concerns. Family members were instructed to place these objects or drawn symbols anywhere in the room, reflecting their perceived distance or connection to the person or experience. Some individuals would place items outside a closed door to symbolize disconnection, while others might position them on top of shelves, inside pockets, or hidden under books. The strategic placement of these objects provided a visual and tangible representation of the family's emotions, offering a means to articulate feelings that were difficult to express verbally.

This exercise often yielded powerful results, enhancing family members' understanding of each other's experiences and fostering increased empathy and patience within the family dynamic. I particularly like the idea of applying this technique to shadow work because it can help us to externalize our thoughts, feelings, and behaviors in a more embodied and creative manner.

EXERCISE: SHADOW CONSTELLATION

In this exercise, we will explore and integrate shadow aspects of the Self by using tarot in a constellation format, which can help uncover hidden relational dynamics and facilitate personal growth. You will need a tarot deck, a large sheet of paper, markers, sticky notes, string or yarn, small objects (such as stones or crystals), and a pen. You can also complete this exercise digitally.

Begin by identifying a shadow you wish to spend time with. This could involve reflecting on suppressed emotions, unacknowledged fears, disowned traits, a recent interaction that triggered you, or a judgment you often make toward others. You can also pull a card if you wish and use that archetype to help you identify a shadow. Once you have identified this shadow, shuffle your tarot deck and pull three additional cards that represent different relationships that might be impacted by this shadow.

Next, map out your constellation. Arrange the selected cards on the paper or around your workspace to represent their relationships and interactions with one another. Pay attention to the spatial arrangement: Are the cards touching, mixed together, or far apart? Use yarn, fabric, crystals, or other meaningful objects to connect or disconnect the cards, visually representing relationships, tensions, and supports. If you prefer, you can draw these connections on paper using different color pens or markers, using solid lines for secure relationships and dotted lines for less secure or strained relationships. To add further symbolism, place small objects—like stones, crystals, or figurines—on or around the cards to symbolize hidden influences, resources, or external pressures. If physical space is limited, you can sketch the card placements on paper and annotate them with words, phrases, or doodles.

To get more in-depth, write key traits, emotions, or roles associated with each card and the relationship it's connected to. This additional context will enrich your constellation. As you observe your creation, ask yourself questions such as What stands in between the cards? Are they connected by other objects? What might the significance of these objects be? Engaging in this reflective process can deepen your understanding of the shadow and facilitate personal growth.

⇒ *Reflect* ⇐

After you have completed your shadow constellation, reflect on the following questions:

- What was your initial reaction to the shadow aspect you chose to explore, and how does it reflect your current relationship with this part of yourself?

- Did any specific card challenge or surprise you as you pulled it? What might that reveal about your internal landscape?

- How do the cards you chose relate to each other, and what roles or archetypes do they seem to embody?

- Which cards do you feel most drawn to or resistant toward, and what does that reveal about your relationship with these parts of yourself?

- How does the spatial arrangement of the cards mirror relationships between parts of yourself, and what do the connections (or lack thereof) symbolize?

- What meanings did you assign to the objects you used, and how do they provide insight into hidden influences or external pressures?

- What shifts in perspective have you experienced regarding your shadow aspect after completing the constellation?

- How can you integrate or address this shadow aspect in your daily life using the insights gained from the exercise?

Chapter 5

Identifying the Shadow through Tarot

❦

*Today, we see the Tarot as a kind of path, a way to personal
growth through understanding of ourselves and life.*

—RACHEL POLLACK

MIRRORS OF THE PSYCHE

The tarot functions as a mirror, reflecting and highlighting the parts of ourselves that we might not easily notice otherwise. Each archetype offers us a deep and expansive view into our own inner world, including our shadows. The Major Arcana, with its archetypal symbols and universal imagery, can serve as a guide through all of the significant stages and lessons of our life's journey. In this sequence, we begin with the potential of the Fool and end with the wisdom and integration of the World. The Major Arcana embodies the universal themes and challenges we all face throughout our life, which is why these cards are beneficial no matter who you are or what stage of life you are in. By utilizing tarot for shadow work, we can uncover the hidden parts of us that lie within these archetypes and learn how to integrate, or assimilate, these shadows so we better understand ourselves and others.

Working with tarot archetypes involves engaging with symbolic representations that can facilitate a deeper understanding of the Self, particularly in recognizing shadow behaviors and traits. Directly listing or contemplating one's own negative characteristics can feel counterproductive and self-defeating. Often, it's easier to observe these undesirable traits in others rather than in ourselves, which is why tarot can be a helpful identifier and buffer in what can otherwise be an uncomfortable process.

Each tarot archetype holds the potential to reflect both a shadow and a golden shadow. Take the Sun, for example. It can represent joy, clarity, and confidence, while also representing the shadow of toxic positivity. Recognizing this duality allows us to hold more than one truth at a time, deepening self-awareness and making self-acceptance more accessible. In her influential workbook *Tarot for Your Self*, Mary K. Greer guides readers on a personalized tarot journey, encouraging them to explore their personality, soul, and hidden factor cards, which contribute to their tarot constellation.

Greer explains that the personality card "indicates what we have come into this particular lifetime to learn" and the soul card "shows your soul purpose through all your lifetime." Additionally, she explains that the hidden factor card, which can be viewed as our shadow or teacher card, represents parts of ourselves that we "fear, reject, or don't see."

I highly recommend reviewing Mary K. Greer's method to calculate your hidden factor card or shadow card. Once you have done this, you can utilize this card for your personal shadow work journey if it aligns with your goals and practice. Or you can simply use it as a means of self-reflection.

Archetypal Shadows

We can think of the Fool as the starting point for this journey, with the bag he carries as a prominent component. In his book *A Little Book on the Human Shadow*, Robert Bly explains that we are born with a metaphorical bag that we carry throughout life. During childhood, parts of ourselves that others (especially caregivers) disapprove of are placed into this bag. Bly describes this developmental process as "bag stuffing" and says it continues into adolescence and adulthood, with messaging now coming from peers instead of caregivers. According to Bly, we spend our early years filling this bag with parts of ourselves that others deem unacceptable, until, by our twenties, we begin the work of emptying it.

This metaphor is particularly well suited to explore the archetype of the Fool through the lens of shadow work. In traditional Rider-Waite-Smith imagery, the Fool is carrying a bag over his shoulder at the start of his journey. If we look at this bag through Bly's theories, then we know that the bag is holding at least twenty years' worth of shadows, and the remaining cards in the deck will help us uncover what they might be.

Tarot can be a powerful tool for exploring the shadow because it allows us to externalize our internal struggles and engage with them in a more tangible, accessible way. Each card serves as a gateway to different aspects of our psyche, inviting us to confront the parts we often hide or ignore. When we pull a card, we are not just interpreting its meaning; we are also opening a dialogue with our inner Self. Repeating cards, in particular, can signal areas of our lives where we may need to spend more time exploring. These cards can serve as reminders to look into the underlying themes associated with our ego, persona, and shadows.

For example, if you consistently pull the Knight of Cups, this could be a nudge to examine how you navigate your emotions, romantic relationships, and the way you approach meaningful connections with others. You might ask yourself, In what ways does the Knight of Cups manifest in my persona or my shadow? In contrast, repeatedly pulling the Six of Wands might invite reflections on your personal achievements, your relationship to recognition, and how you handle validation in your life. You might ask yourself, In what ways does the Six of Wands manifest in my persona or my shadow? This exploration can help you identify how these archetypal influences affect your experiences and interactions.

Engaging with tarot in this way encourages us to see the delicate relationships between our ego, persona, and shadow. By acknowledging the roles these components play in our lives, we can start to unpack the complexities of our identity. The persona, representing the social mask we wear, often tries to hide the shadow's influence. Tarot helps us illuminate these connections, guiding us toward a more balanced Self.

The remainder of this chapter focuses on how the Major Arcana may represent aspects of both the shadow and the golden shadow. As you move through each interpretation, consider how you might embody these qualities or, conversely, recall instances where you have felt upset by similar traits in others. Reflecting on both ends of the spectrum (qualities you admire and those you reject) can deepen your understanding of the shadow's influence on your life. Allow these archetypes to serve as mirrors, revealing parts of yourself that may need acknowledgment, acceptance, or integration. Please keep in mind, tarot is inherently projective, and as a tool for healing, it should be viewed through a flexible lens. While these are interpretations that make sense to me and have been influenced by my work as a psychotherapist, you have your own relationship to these cards and may have entirely different shadow associations. This is why tarot is such an accessible, universal tool. I encourage you to take notes about your own thoughts regarding these archetypes as shadows.

THE FOOL

The shadow side of the Fool can show up as avoiding responsibilities or running away from problems instead of facing them. This kind of behavior can cause chaos in someone's life by sabotaging relationships, creating internal and external instability, and lead to missed opportunities for growth and connection. This shadow can also be driven by a constant need for excitement or change, which can come from being afraid to settle down or commit.

On the other hand, the golden shadow of the Fool is about being open to new experiences and ideas. It reflects a deep trust in the journey of life and a belief that every step (good or bad) can help us grow and better understand ourselves.

REFLECT

- In what ways are you avoiding responsibilities or escaping from reality?

- How does your lack of planning impact your life, relationships, and goals?

- In what ways are you open to new ideas and experiences?

- How can you foster deeper trust in the process of life?

THE MAGICIAN

The shadow of the Magician can be manipulative, in order to fool others or to avoid being honest with themselves. With this shadow, someone might pretend to have it all together on the outside, while behind the scenes they are avoiding responsibility or deeper self-reflection. Instead of using their skills to grow or create real change, they use them to protect their image or avoid vulnerability. This shadow can stem from a fear of not being good enough, so they try to control how others see them instead of honoring their authentic self.

The golden shadow of the Magician is innovative, creative, resourceful, and willing to be seen. This aspect of the Magician loves to experiment, often uncovering fresh possibilities and ideas that others might overlook. Driven by curiosity and courage, this golden shadow embraces personal potential and is willing to be seen for who they really are.

REFLECT

- In what ways might you be manipulating yourself?

- When do you tend to use your skills or resources to manipulate situations or people to achieve your own goals?

- When do you feel most connected to your creative and innovative potential?

- When was the last time you took a risk or experimented with something new?

THE HIGH PRIESTESS

The shadow of the High Priestess can show up as being aloof, avoidant, or emotionally unavailable. As a shadow, the High Priestess is detached and engages in spiritual bypassing, where they use spirituality or mysticism to avoid facing real emotions or hard truths, like saying "everything happens for a reason" instead of dealing with pain or conflict. This shadow may have developed from growing up in an environment where emotions and experiences were dismissed, shamed, or punished.

The golden shadow of the High Priestess values depth and meaning. As a golden shadow, the High Priestess is comfortable sitting with the unknown and sharing meaningful, necessary truths with those who seek it.

REFLECT

- In what areas of your life do you find yourself keeping secrets or withholding important information from others?

- What personal truths are you avoiding acknowledging within yourself?

- How might you bring a sense of intentionality and care to the insights you share with others?

- What practices might help you deepen your trust in your own inner guidance?

THE EMPRESS

The shadow of the Empress is selfish and impatient. They might find excuses to avoid their obligations and responsibilities because they feel entitled. The impatience of the Empress can create a sense of frustration when things don't go the way they want them to, which can result in this shadow abandoning projects, goals, or relationships that require time, care, and attention to grow. This shadow might stem from being devalued as a child or experiencing inconsistent caregiving.

The golden shadow of the Empress is concerned with the well-being of others and seeks to provide assistance whenever they can, while still tending to themselves in the process. This golden shadow also values creativity and pleasure.

REFLECT

- When you think about your obligations and responsibilities, what excuses do you make to avoid them?

- Where in your life do you find yourself being impatient or focused on your own needs to the detriment of others?

- In what ways do you value creativity and pleasure?

- How can you continue to cultivate your ability to care for others without losing sight of your own needs?

THE EMPEROR

THE EMPEROR.

The shadow of the Emperor is tyrannical and self-absorbed. They need power and control and are willing to do whatever is needed to obtain it. This shadow often stems from a deep fear of vulnerability or unpredictability, which drives the Emperor to build a rigid boundary of control that isolates them from true connection and collaboration with others.

The golden shadow of the Emperor is assertive and seeks stability for themselves and others. They find value in order, predictability, and structure without demanding it from others, instead seeking guidance and inviting suggestions from others. If the shadow of the Emperor is authoritarian, then the golden shadow is authoritative.

REFLECT

- In what areas of your life do you find yourself needing to exert excessive control or dominance?

- What fears or insecurities might be driving this need for power?

- How does having a clear sense of order, structure, and predictability benefit you and those around you?

- How can you ensure that your leadership is rooted in mutual respect and care?

THE HIEROPHANT

The shadow of the Hierophant can be judgmental and intolerant of others who have different thoughts, beliefs, customs, or ways of living. This may result in a dogmatic attitude in which opposing ideas are viewed as dangerous or "wrong." This shadow may develop from experiencing environments where conformity was necessary for safety and belonging.

As a golden shadow, the Hierophant shows respect for the paths others take that are different from their own. Rather than being critical, the Hierophant has the ability to guide others with compassion, curiosity, and a sincere intention to assist them in discovering their own personal truths.

REFLECT

- When have you been judgmental or intolerant of others' beliefs or practices?

- How do you typically react when confronted with ideas or customs that challenge your own?

- How can you create space for others to find their own truth, rather than imposing your ideas onto them?

- What practices can help you stay grounded while embracing diversity of thought and belief?

THE LOVERS

The shadow of the Lovers can show up as being controlling or inflexible, especially when it comes to relationships and decision-making. Instead of creating space for reciprocal authentic connections, this shadow tends to push their own personal wants and desires onto others and can struggle with compromise. Deep down, this shadow is often afraid of vulnerability, both with others and with themselves. This shadow might stem from experiencing conditional love, boundary violations, or emotional betrayal.

As a golden shadow, the Lovers archetype will enthusiastically invite different parts of themselves to coexist while actively celebrating their own and others' diversity. In relationships, this golden shadow understands the value of autonomy, self-expression, and mutual respect.

REFLECT

- What aspects of yourself do you resist exploring or acknowledging?

- When have you imposed your desires onto a partner without regard for their needs?

- How can you invite different parts of yourself to coexist harmoniously?

- How do you promote autonomy and mutual respect in your relationships with others?

THE CHARIOT

The shadow of the Chariot is contradictory, often oscillating between conflicting thoughts, feelings, and behaviors. They can be unpredictable and chaotic, choosing not to commit to any one thought, idea, or decision, which often leaves those closest to them frustrated. Covered in armor and protected by sphinxes, the Chariot as a shadow also avoids vulnerability and refuses to ask for help from others. This shadow may stem from being shamed for asking for help or from experiencing a lack of safety and stability.

As a golden shadow, the Chariot is helpful, optimistic, and confident in their direction in life and decision-making. This golden shadow, while confident and secure, still values and invites insight and help from others when necessary.

REFLECT

- In what areas of your life do you experience internal conflict or contradictory behaviors, and how do they manifest?

- What feelings emerge when you consider opening yourself to vulnerability?

- When you imagine yourself as confident and aligned in your direction in life, how does this image differ from your current experience?

- What steps can you take to shift from a place of avoidance and chaos to one of confidence and balance?

STRENGTH

The shadow of Strength lacks boundaries and emotional awareness. This archetype will avoid standing up for themselves and denies addressing the presence of difficult emotions like anger and aggression. This shadow is also rooted in feelings of inadequacy and may have stemmed from experiencing rejection or punishment for self-advocacy and emotional expression.

As a golden shadow, Strength understands the inherent discomfort in difficult emotions but still acknowledges their existence. This archetypal golden shadow is calm, centered, and gentle—even in moments of tension and discomfort.

REFLECT

- In what areas of your life do you notice a tendency to avoid setting boundaries or asserting yourself?

- How do you typically respond to personal feelings of anger or aggression?

- In what ways could you begin to embody a calm, centered presence even in moments of tension?

- What would it look like if you acknowledged discomfort while remaining grounded?

THE HERMIT

The shadow of the Hermit dismisses the benefits of connection with others. This archetypal
shadow refuses help, guidance, or compan-
ionship because they view it as a distraction.
The Hermit as a shadow can be arrogant
and judgmental toward others who think differently than they do or don't show value or
interest in the Hermit's level of introspection.
This shadow may form after being excluded,
judged, and abandoned, creating the belief
that self-containment and isolation are safer
than connection.

As a golden shadow, the Hermit stands
steady amidst the chaos of the outside world. They understand the value
in both learning from others and staying true to oneself. While this golden
shadow prioritizes the inner needs of the Self, they are still mindful of the
needs and unique experiences of others.

REFLECT

- When do you tend to dismiss the value of connection and
  support from others?

- When are you most likely to be judgmental or dismissive of
  the ideas or perspectives of others?

- How do you balance your need for solitude with the necessity
  of maintaining meaningful connections?

- How can you remain true to yourself while being open to
  learning from others?

WHEEL OF FORTUNE

: WHEEL OF FORTUNE. 4

There are two aspects to the shadow of the Wheel of Fortune. One seeks to control outcomes and manipulate circumstances to avoid feelings of ambiguity and uncertainty. The other seeks to avoid any personal responsibility by instead becoming overly reliant on the concept of fate. This shadow can form when personal agency is either overemphasized (creating guilt when things go wrong) or completely dismissed (creating learned helplessness), resulting in the individual developing an imbalanced relationship with power, effort, and outcomes.

As a golden shadow, the Wheel of Fortune embraces ambiguity by welcoming the inherent uncertainty of life and practices being open to what these experiences could offer in terms of growth and healing. The golden shadow motto of the Wheel of Fortune is "Trust the process."

REFLECT

- In what ways are you resistant to ambiguity?

- In what ways do you try to control or manipulate outcomes?

- How do you feel when you are going with the flow of life?

- What does it look like when you are trusting the process?

JUSTICE

As a shadow, Justice is harshly rigid when it comes to rules, leaving no room for nuance or flexibility. This shadow can be aggressively judgmental and critical of anyone who strays from what they believe to be the correct path or way of doing something. The shadow of Justice often forms when love or approval was tied to being "good" or "right." To feel safe, this shadow clings to rigid rules and becomes judgmental toward others who do not follow them.

As a golden shadow, Justice has a deep appreciation for equity and equality and uses this appreciation and understanding to advocate for themself and others.

REFLECT

- In what ways do you harshly judge others when it comes to rules and expectations?

- What are you afraid will happen if you let go of your need to control or impose justice in every situation?

- What aspects of your life demonstrate that you have a strong moral compass, and how can you more fully live in alignment with that wisdom?

- How can you leverage your understanding of balance to create harmony within yourself and your relationships?

THE HANGED ONE

The shadow of the Hanged One is resistant to new or differing perspectives. This shadow is marked by feelings of pride and stubbornness as well, often avoiding opportunities for self-reflection. This shadow believes there is no need to change their current ways of thinking and being. This shadow may stem from experiencing shame, guilt, or punishment for sharing their personal perspective, which can lead to a rigid sense of identity or belief system tied to self-preservation.

As a golden shadow, the Hanged One finds value in seeing different perspectives and seeks out opportunities that promote growth and change even if it's uncomfortable. The Hanged One's golden shadow motto is "A comfort zone is a beautiful place, but nothing ever grows there."

REFLECT

- When does your pride get in the way of being curious about different perspectives?

- How does your reluctance to embrace discomfort or uncertainty lead to feeling stuck or stagnant?

- How can you invite more openness to new ways of thinking and understanding, especially in challenging situations?

- What might you learn by embracing discomfort instead of avoiding it?

DEATH

The shadow of the Death card reflects a deep avoidance of endings and a resistance to change. As a shadow, this archetype may show up as an unwillingness to release that which has outlived its purpose, which may include relationships, habits, routines, or beliefs. This shadow often views change through pessimistic lenses, refusing to acknowledge opportunities for growth. This shadow may form due to overexposure to comfort and emotional reactivity to suggested change.

As a golden shadow, the Death archetype views endings and change as a powerful opportunity for personal transformation. This golden shadow of Death accepts the inevitable cycles of life and death from both a literal and a metaphorical viewpoint. This golden shadow actively invites change and transformation.

REFLECT

- In what ways do you struggle to release what no longer serves you, even when you know it's time to move on?

- How can you reframe your fear of endings to view them as opportunities for renewal and growth?

- How can you practice trusting the process of transformation, even when it feels uncomfortable or uncertain?

- How can you better honor the cycles of death and rebirth in your life?

TEMPERANCE

The shadow of Temperance struggles to navigate the complexities of duality, often resulting in cognitive distortions like all-or-nothing thinking. This shadow forms when someone learns that it's not safe or acceptable to feel conflicting emotions or live in a "gray area." So they default to all-or-nothing thinking where they see people, situations, or even themselves as either totally good or totally bad, right or wrong. For this shadow, holding space for "both/and" feels too unstable, so they cling to "either/or."

As a golden shadow, Temperance seeks to embrace the process of blending and mixing, while equally holding space for anything that may be in opposition of each other. This golden shadow acknowledges and celebrates the ability to have more than one experience or feeling at the same time, such as joy and sorrow, or certainty and doubt.

REFLECT

- In what ways do you find yourself thinking in absolutes, and how does this impact your relationships and experiences?

- How can you practice acknowledging and embracing the dualities present in your life without feeling overwhelmed?

- What are some examples of situations where you have successfully navigated and embraced the concept of duality?

- How can you foster an attitude of curiosity and openness toward the complexity of your emotions and the experiences of others?

THE DEVIL

The shadow of the Devil relies heavily on maladaptive coping mechanisms and gravitates toward quick fixes, often impulsively. This shadow lacks personal accountability, often blaming others for their decisions, experiences, and feelings. This shadow often forms from experiencing shame and a loss of personal agency.

As a golden shadow, the Devil recognizes their triggers and seeks alternative methods of coping that align with their overall well-being, while still acknowledging the willpower it takes to accomplish this.

REFLECT

- What unhealthy attachments, coping mechanisms, or habits do you engage in, and what steps can you take to address them?

- Where might you be avoiding personal accountability?

- How can you practice self-compassion and patience?

- What alternative methods of coping can you experiment with?

THE TOWER

THE TOWER.

The shadow of the Tower revels in chaos and is known to "stir the pot." This shadow will engage in destructive behavior for personal gain and deny any involvement or accountability. This shadow also focuses on inner turmoil but refuses to implement change while holding on to outdated and unhelpful belief systems. This shadow may form when a person experiences a false sense of connection with others through shared chaos (such as gossip, bullying, drama, or mutual criticism). In these moments, destruction becomes a substitute for intimacy and bonding.

As a golden shadow, the Tower is unafraid to dismantle archaic structures in order to build newer, inclusive spaces, both internally and externally. This golden shadow highlights the value in letting go of what no longer serves them.

REFLECT

- What outdated beliefs, structures, or relationships are you holding on to, and why are you afraid to let them go?

- In what areas of your life do you tend to "stir the pot"? What do you gain by doing this?

- What parts of yourself or your life are asking to be torn down?

- How can you honor the role of destruction as a natural part of your personal evolution?

THE STAR

The shadow of the Star represents a deep fear of vulnerability and a reluctance to fully express one's true Self. As a shadow, the Star does everything in its power to avoid being seen, perceived, or acknowledged. This fear of being seen can lead to isolation, stagnation, and a deep sense of inadequacy. The shadow of the Star often forms when someone has experienced rejection, ridicule, or emotional wounding after moments of openness or self-expression.

As a golden shadow, the Star embodies openness and trust. This archetype respects the healing power of vulnerability and knows that healing comes from embracing one's whole Self, flaws and all. The golden shadow of the Star tends to their discomfort of being seen while gently guiding the Self toward experiences that foster connection, compassion, and self-acceptance.

REFLECT

- In what ways do you hide your true Self or suppress your emotions out of fear of being judged or rejected?

- How has your fear of vulnerability impacted your ability to form meaningful connections with others?

- How can you reframe vulnerability as a strength rather than a weakness, allowing yourself to embrace authenticity in your relationships and creative pursuits?

- In what ways are you holding back from pursuing your dreams or expressing your inner truth?

THE MOON

The shadow of the Moon perpetuates a pattern of denial and avoidance of the truth. The shadow of the Moon forms when emotional or psychological truths have been deemed too overwhelming. This leads to the development of coping mechanisms rooted in personal denial, distortion, or projection.

The golden shadow of the Moon embraces transparency and honesty and understands the value in exploring and sharing the discoveries within the subconscious. This golden shadow prioritizes honesty with the Self and others regarding their thoughts, needs, and fears.

REFLECT

- Where in your life are you withholding information from yourself or others, and why are you afraid to reveal the truth?

- How does your tendency to keep secrets or avoid vulnerability prevent you from forming deeper, more authentic connections?

- How can you practice being more transparent with others, and what benefits might arise from sharing more of your authentic Self?

- What hidden strengths or insights might you uncover by exploring your subconscious mind without fear or resistance?

THE SUN

The shadow of the Sun is rooted in toxic positivity. This shadow is overly focused on presenting a successful image to the outside world and focuses on seeking happiness and external validation through materialistic and superficial endeavors. This shadow is shallow, attention-seeking, and has an intense fear of "being exposed" as a fraud or imposter. The shadow of the Sun often forms when a person learns that being accepted, loved, or valued depends on appearing happy, successful, or "together" at all times.

As a golden shadow, the Sun understands the balance between searching for inner happiness and personal success, while also embracing the inevitably of failure and hardship. The Sun as a golden shadow can acknowledge both the good and the bad in any situation without neglecting authenticity.

REFLECT

- Where in your life do you feel pressure to appear perfect or successful?

- In what ways do you embody toxic positivity?

- In what areas of your life are you sacrificing authenticity for the sake of maintaining an idealized image?

- How can you cultivate joy and confidence from within, independent of external validation or recognition?

JUDGEMENT

The shadow of Judgement is marked by a crippling fear of making mistakes or being scrutinized for current or past decisions, which inevitably leads to living a life driven by guilt, shame, or the perceived need to meet unrealistic expectations. This shadow often seeks external validation and approval due to an inability to trust themselves, which increases feelings of unworthiness or inadequacy. This shadow forms when someone learns that mistakes lead to rejection, shame, or punishment, rather than growth.

As a golden shadow, Judgement is willing to acknowledge past mistakes or decisions and view them as moments of learning and growth rather than as a source of guilt. This golden shadow understands the importance of accountability and restoration with the Self and others.

REFLECT

- Where in your life are you being overly critical of yourself, and how does this self-judgment prevent you from moving forward?

- What past mistakes or regrets are you holding on to, and how can you begin to let them go while maintaining accountability?

- How can you begin to forgive yourself for past missteps and see them as opportunities for growth rather than as sources of shame or guilt?

- How can you cultivate a sense of self-compassion and acceptance, allowing you to embrace both your strengths and your imperfections?

THE WORLD

The shadow of the World is rooted in a feeling that no matter what is achieved, it's not enough. Instead of celebrating accomplishments and embracing new beginnings, the shadow of the World stays stuck ruminating about the past and thinking about what could be in the future. This shadow perpetuates feelings of emptiness and apathy. This shadow forms when someone learns that even their biggest accomplishments are not truly valued or acknowledged, or when success is always met with the question "What's next?"

As a golden shadow, the World enthusiastically seeks integration with all of their complex and dynamic parts. This golden shadow revels in their accomplishments no matter how small and feels content in their life journey.

REFLECT

- In what areas of your life do you struggle to feel a sense of completion or satisfaction, even after achieving something meaningful?

- How might your tendency to focus on past events prevent you from embracing new beginnings or celebrating your progress?

- How can you begin to welcome and integrate the complex parts of yourself that you may have overlooked or dismissed?

- How can you cultivate a sense of fulfillment that is not dependent on external achievements or validation?

THE SUITS AS SHADOWS

While the Major Arcana offers us valuable archetypal shadows, the Minor Arcana and suits do as well. By understanding the suits as shadows, we can better identify patterns in our thoughts, feelings, and behaviors. In this section, we will explore each suit through the lens of its shadow and consider how these archetypal energies can both hinder and foster growth on the journey to individuation. By acknowledging the shadow aspects of the suits, we can deepen our relationship with the cards, ourselves, and those around us.

The court cards also hold valuable shadow insights. From a developmental perspective, the Pages are deeply connected to childhood and adolescence—key periods when our shadows begin to form. As we progress through life, the Knights, Queens, and Kings serve as archetypal markers of early, middle, and late adulthood respectively, each representing different stages of shadow formation and development. Consider exploring these court cards alongside the suits to offer a comprehensive view of how shadow material has evolved and impacted you throughout your life journey thus far.

Cups

 In its shadow form, the suit of Cups reflects fear and avoidance of vulnerability, along with an inability to establish healthy emotional boundaries with others. The shadow of the Cups can also find itself floating in codependent behaviors by sacrificing their own emotional needs to keep the peace or please others.

As a golden shadow, the suit of Cups embodies healthy emotional boundaries, values emotional awareness, and views emotional vulnerability as a strength. This golden shadow is nurturing and validating of others, but also takes time to hold space for and tend to their own needs.

REFLECT

- What emotions have you been repressing, and how might you begin to explore them in a safe and healthy way?

- How can you create more balanced emotional connections, where both giving and receiving are equal and nurturing?

Wands

As a shadow, the suit of Wands is impulsive and reckless. This shadow is driven by instant gratification and doesn't consider possible outcomes or consequences when making a decision. They are often told that they "act without thinking." The shadow of the Wands believes slowing down is a sign of weakness or defeat.

As a golden shadow, the suit of Wands celebrates their energy and inspiration while acknowledging the benefit of slower, measured pursuits. This golden shadow values a strong forward motion but is still mindful of the potential impacts and consequences of their decisions.

REFLECT

- Where in your life are you acting impulsively and without regard to consequences?

- What steps can you take to bring more mindfulness and consideration to your actions?

Swords

The shadow of the Swords is rooted in self-sabotage. This shadow is often stuck in negative thought loops that accentuate feelings of fear and inadequacy. As a shadow, the Swords are overly reliant on logic and refuse to seek balance in their thinking and approach to situations in which nuance is important.

As a golden shadow, the Swords value insight and seek clarity through the gathering of information to make appropriate and healthy decisions. This golden shadow suit embodies clear and effective communication, fairness, and the willingness to face difficult truths with integrity and curiosity.

REFLECT

- How do you use logic or intellect as a defense mechanism to avoid vulnerability or emotional truth?

- How can you begin to balance your logical mind with your emotional mind?

Pentacles

 As a shadow, the suit of Pentacles is selfish, greedy, and materialistic. This suit will hoard resources and prioritize personal gain over collective well-being. The shadow of the Pentacles is also overly concerned with their external image and will inflate their wealth or status in order to be perceived favorably by others.

As a golden shadow, the suit of Pentacles seeks balance between obtaining resources for the Self and sharing with the community. This golden shadow values hard work and discipline but recognizes the need for, and importance of, a healthy work/life balance.

REFLECT

- In what areas of your life are you overly focused on material success, and how is this impacting your personal growth or relationships?

- How can you create a more balanced relationship with your resources, using them mindfully and with purpose rather than out of fear or insecurity?

Chapter 6

The Ancestral Shadow

Trauma decontextualized in a person looks like personality.
Trauma decontextualized in a family looks like family traits.
Trauma decontextualized in a people looks like culture.

—Resmaa Menakem

WHAT IS PASSED DOWN

In addition to our individual shadows, we also harbor ancestral or generational shadows. The ancestral shadow is material that belongs to our family system and has originated as recently as our parents or further back, extending even beyond great-great-grandparents. This type of shadow functions similarly to the concept of generational trauma. Generational trauma, also referred to as ancestral or intergenerational trauma, encompasses the emotional and psychological wounds that are passed down through families. These traumas often originate from adverse experiences had by family members or ancestors, which subsequently influence their emotions, beliefs, coping mechanisms, and overall behavior. These influences then shape the development of other family members' mental, emotional, and psychological functioning based on how they interact with us, leading to learned behavior and internalizing covert or overt messaging.

In fact, a 2005 study on transgenerational effects of posttraumatic stress disorder highlighted the importance of epigenetics and found that there are biological changes in the children of individuals who have experienced trauma. These findings suggest that despite never having experienced a specific trauma, children can still exhibit symptoms of that trauma due to genetic imprinting. This means that the emotional wounds and maladaptive coping mechanisms of one generation end up becoming the unconsciously inherited shadow of the next. We can think about this through the visual of nesting dolls. We are the outermost doll, and each different doll descending in size is separate from us, yet still exists within us.

In my clinical practice, I frequently illustrate this process of generational trauma with a specific example. Consider a client with an intense fear of fire, despite having no direct personal experience with a traumatic fire-related event. Through deeper exploration, it's discovered that the client's mother prohibited candles in the home due to her own fear of fire. This behavior is traced back further to the client's grandmother, who exhibited a similar fear, reacting with anxiety and reprimanding the client's mother whenever a candle was lit or when the kitchen stove became too hot. Ultimately, it's uncovered that the client's great-grandmother was a victim of a house fire as a young child and subsequently banned open flames in or around her home. This example shows how an ancestor's trauma was passed down through generations, affecting members of the family without them having experienced the trauma themselves.

This same concept can be applied to the concept of the ancestral shadow. An example of an ancestral shadow could be hyper-independence. If we apply the shadows of tarot, we might label this shadow the Queen of Swords. While hyper-independence often emerges as a trauma response to unmet emotional needs in childhood, we can still view it through the lens of the shadow if it formed from being rejected for asking for help. When caregivers fail to nurture or respond appropriately to a child's needs (by dismissing emotional expression, discouraging vulnerability, or even punishing basic requests for care), the child internalizes the belief that expressing needs or desires is inherently wrong, bad, or burdensome. These early experiences give rise to deep-rooted narratives, such as "I am too much" or "I am a burden," which serve as protective mechanisms against further emotional rejection.

From a developmental perspective, children are not capable of recognizing the complexities of their caregivers' limitations; instead, they assume that their own perceived inadequacies are to blame. As a result, hyper-independence becomes a trauma response and defense mechanism. The child learns to suppress emotional needs and begins to pride themselves on self-sufficiency, never seeking help and assuming full responsibility for managing their emotions and challenges alone. This is when the shadow develops. In this example, the child internalizes the belief that having needs is undesirable, leading them to suppress these needs, which becomes a foundation for shadow material. As this material remains unacknowledged, it may manifest as projection in adulthood, where the individual experiences irritation or frustration toward others who openly express their needs.

If this trauma remains unacknowledged throughout adulthood, it can infiltrate various relational spheres, from friendships and romantic partnerships to professional environments and manifest as a shadow. When emotional needs arise within these relationships and are not fully met, the individual may retreat, reinforcing the deeply ingrained belief that needing others is both problematic and risky. The unresolved pain of feeling like they are "too much" then becomes a recurring trigger, contributing to cycles of withdrawal and emotional isolation, even in the face of genuine care from others.

Hyper-independence, therefore, can be understood as a manifestation of the ancestral shadow—patterns of emotional suppression and avoidance that are passed down through family systems. These inherited defense mechanisms reflect the broader generational wounds of emotional deprivation, neglect, or trauma that haven't been healed.

Working with the ancestral shadow can feel overwhelming. One challenge is that we may lack the information, memories, or family connections needed to fully understand where this shadow material is rooted. Additionally, many people feel uneasy about engaging with ancestors or ancestral trauma due to the problematic behaviors, beliefs, and values of past generations that they do not agree with. This is understandable and if that type of shadow work does not align with you, then that is completely fine.

GENERATIONAL MESSAGING

Much of my work as a therapist includes stories. Some stories belong to us, but there are plenty that don't, yet we carry them around as if they do. It would be impossible for me to keep track of the number of times I have asked clients, "Where did that story originate?" More often than not, they tell me it started in childhood and came from a parent, family member, teacher, religious leader, or some other figure of authority in their life. However, stories continue to form throughout our lives and into adulthood and can still be formed by these same people. Except now stories are shaped by not only our family but by our coworkers, boss, partners, neighbors, and social media.

We often don't realize that these stories that have been written based on significant influences in our life actually have roots that extend far beyond the present. Think about the incredible way a forest develops. Trees can speak to each other, care for each other, or make each other sick solely based on their buried root system. This complex network of roots connects them all, sometimes spanning vast distances beneath the surface. In a similar way, the stories we carry are like those roots. They intertwine and entangle with the stories of those who came before us, shaping our perception of ourselves and the world. These stories, much like the roots, can either nourish us, providing strength and stability, or they can harm us, limiting our growth and preventing us from accessing our full potential.

Just as trees adapt by shedding dead leaves and branches, or even by seeking better nutrients from other, healthier trees nearby, we too have the ability to adapt and even re-root. This process requires us to first examine the roots that hold us in place, such as the beliefs, narratives, and patterns we have inherited, and ask ourselves whether they truly serve us. Are they stories that bring us growth or hinder our growth?

When we recognize that some of our deepest stories are not our own, we give ourselves permission to dig deeper and uproot them. This might mean challenging the narratives that were passed down by parents, or reexamining lessons taught by teachers or mentors that no longer align with who we are today. The act of re-rooting is not about erasing these stories, but rather understanding their origins and deciding whether we want to carry them forward.

This metaphor of re-rooting invites us to imagine what it would look like to uproot and then replant ourselves in new, fertile soil. What happens when we let go of stories that no longer serve us? What new narratives can we cultivate, and how might those stories allow us to grow into our fullest potential? Much like a tree that thrives when given the right conditions, we too can grow strong and resilient when we nurture the stories that truly belong to us, while acknowledging the ones that have impacted us, and allowing them to break off and become absorbed by the earth.

BREAKING THE ANCESTRAL SHADOW CYCLE

I was working with a client who initially started therapy because most of their friends were in therapy, and they felt it was something they were "supposed" to do at that point in their life. At first, they presented with no major concerns, but eventually acknowledged that discussing their feelings was not their strong suit and in fact made them very uncomfortable. They also shared that when others expressed emotions around them, their instinct was either to laugh or to want to avoid the situation entirely. This was where our work began.

Through our time together, the client unearthed a generational shadow—as a child, they grew up in a family where emotional expression was discouraged and often met with negativity or punishment. The client recalled always remembering being told to go to their room if they were crying or upset about something. Over time, this repeated scenario started to form a shadow narrative that consisted of messages such as "If I show emotion, I'll be abandoned or punished" and "Having emotions is a sign of weakness."

We began to explore the root system of this shadow. This client had never met their grandmother as she had passed prior to the client's birth, but they remembered hearing stories about her being "cold, aloof, and harsh." The client and I then explored how if parents, due to their own upbringing, learned to suppress their emotions—perhaps as a means of survival—they can often unconsciously teach their children the same behavior. In this case, the child then internalizes the message that emotions are undesirable or problematic, which begins the process of emotional repression. This is how the foundation of their ancestral shadow material is constructed and thus begins a cycle of them abandoning their own emotional needs and vulnerabilities.

In patterns such as this, the child then becomes an adult with an unexamined ancestral shadow that manifests through projection—perhaps they become annoyed or irritated when a friend, partner, or their own child expresses emotion. They also become increasingly reluctant to connect emotionally with others, which inevitably has a negative effect on the quality of their relationships.

This client's focus eventually turned to healing the parts that felt unseen, and they worked hard to acknowledge this ancestral shadow. The client found ways to cultivate compassion for their grandmother by creating tea-drinking rituals based on a specific childhood memory. They often remembered watching their mother steep tea and sit at the kitchen table, gazing out the window. They remembered their mother talking about how much their grandmother drank tea. In our sessions, while we acknowledged that they could never truly know what their mother or grandmother was thinking, the client could still allow themself to imagine compassionate possibilities. Maybe their mother was daydreaming about a creative project, wondering about her child's future, or simply trying to process her own overwhelming emotions as a mother. Perhaps she was even mourning her own mother's inability to tend to her emotions as a child and adult.

The client's tea-drinking ritual gradually became more involved to include specific blends tailored to their emotional state and grew to include personal mantras before and after the tea ritual. Eventually the client began to write letters to their mother and grandmother, sharing the deep, emotional well of life experiences they were never able to share with them growing up. While their mother had passed away several years before, they used this ritual as an opportunity to connect with their mother and grandmother in ways they were never afforded. This practice eventually paved the way for the client to increase their own capacity to hold space for the emotions of others, which led to stronger relationships with friends, family, and romantic partners.

EXERCISE: RE-ROOTING THE SHADOW

The purpose of this exercise is to explore deep-seated beliefs and narratives that may stem from generational trauma and to examine how they can be transformed. Begin by visualizing yourself as a tree. Close your eyes and imagine your roots extending deep into the earth, connecting with the roots of your ancestors. As you hold this image, ask yourself, "What stories or beliefs have my roots inherited, absorbed, or become entangled with?" Allow anything that comes to mind to surface, even if it seems insignificant or abstract, and write it down.

Next, choose one belief or narrative that feels particularly significant. Reflect on its origin and consider whether this belief has served and nourished you, or if it feels like it is preventing your growth. Once you have examined this inherited belief, visualize replanting your roots in new, fertile soil. Take time to write about the new belief or narrative you would like to grow in place of the old one. You may also choose to pull a tarot card or two to help guide you in this exercise.

Chapter 7

Integrating the Shadow

There is no generally effective technique for assimilating the shadow. It is more like diplomacy or statesmanship and it is always an individual matter. First one has to accept and take seriously the existence of the shadow. Second, one has to become aware of its qualities and intentions. This happens through conscientious attention to moods, fantasies and impulses. Third, a long process of negotiation is unavoidable.

—CARL JUNG

ASSIMILATION

When we reach the point of shadow assimilation, we are inviting the repressed or rejected parts of ourselves back into our conscious awareness so that we can work with the material in our everyday life. Ideally, this process helps to decrease our reactivity to the behaviors exhibited by others that trigger, or hook, one of our own shadows. Shadow integration is vital to living as a well-adjusted individual. When we don't explore or identify the shadow, we are unable to acknowledge our own blind spots that cloud the way we view the world or show up in relationships. This inevitably limits our ability to truly connect with others and experience our full potential.

Identifying, acknowledging, and then integrating the shadow allows us to access a deeper layer of compassion and empathy, not only for ourselves, but also for those around us. It's important to note that there is no specific protocol or process for shadow integration, or what Jung referred to as assimilation. This process functions more as increased self-awareness and is unique to everyone. However, there are some universal steps that can be taken to help with assimilating the shadow.

One step in this process is increasing our overall level of self-awareness and cultivating a healthy dose of curiosity regarding the way we show up or react in a variety of situations. Simply engaging in the exercises throughout this book, reflecting on your own emotions, behaviors, and experiences, expands and exercises your mind and awareness. For example, much of this process has included the act of recognizing behavioral patterns we dislike or disown about ourselves. Before we engaged in shadow work, these behaviors might have triggered intense emotional reactions like anger or frustration, leading to impulsive and reactive responses. These heightened emotions often arise because these traits we have acknowledged have been deemed "bad" and are usually judged harshly by ourselves and others, creating a strong aversion to them. However, through the integration and assimilation process, we no longer beat ourselves up. We can acknowledge we have the capacity to think, feel, or behave in a way that may be unfavorable and work to make healthy, safe decisions without berating ourselves in the process.

Integrating the shadow does not mean that we are giving ourselves permission to engage in the behaviors we have repressed, nor does it mean that we now approve of these behaviors—we now will just have the ability to be less triggered and controlled by them. Integration involves acknowledging these tendencies as part of the human experience while consciously choosing not to be reactive toward them and instead simply be aware of them. There is so much power in noticing a shadow, a feeling, or the urge to react and then choosing to be curious about it instead. This self-awareness fosters a more measured, compassionate response when confronted with our shadow.

We can expand on the concept of integration, or shadow assimilation, by spending time with the archetypes of the World, the Lovers, and the Aces in tarot. In traditional interpretations, the Lovers card often symbolizes a romantic partnership, but limiting this archetype to such a literal interpretation overlooks its deeper, more nuanced meaning. While it certainly can represent relationships, this card embodies far more than that.

At its core, the Lovers archetype is about duality and the idea that two different or even conflicting things can both be true. This mirrors a key concept from Dialectical Behavior Therapy (DBT), which teaches that personal growth comes from accepting complexity. The Lovers reflects the inner tension we feel between the various parts of ourselves—like the version we show the world (the persona) and the parts we hide (the shadow), or between different wants and values. While these parts might seem at odds, they are all a valid and unavoidable part of being human. When we are able to hold space for this "both/and" mentality, we become more whole and content.

This is where the energy of "choice," a concept often associated with the Lovers archetype, comes into play. The Lovers challenges us to choose self-acceptance and integration, to step beyond the fear of judgment and say, "I am not just one thing. I have a multitude of passions, interests, and identities, and shadows, and that is perfectly okay." There is a hidden permission within the Lovers, one that invites us to step outside our shadows and perceived limitations in order to embrace the different facets of our identity. This choice, though it may seem daunting, grants us the freedom to coexist with our many parts without constant tension or conflict.

The Aces in tarot offer a powerful archetypal system for exploring the duality within our identities and inner world. Take the Ace of Swords for example: it invites deep introspection and clarity around the internal conflict that often arises when confronting our shadows. As we engage in shadow work, different aspects of the Self inevitably surface, sometimes clashing with one another.

For example, we may feel split between the roles of being a responsible parent or employee by day and a passionate artist or tarot reader by night. In the case of shadow work, it might be revealed that while we might value kindness, we still have the capacity to lash out in traffic or feel tempted to gossip. Discomfort emerges when we see these opposing aspects as incompatible, believing we must choose one over the other. This inner fragmentation, when unacknowledged, can fuel anxiety and depression. Here, the archetype of the Lovers becomes relevant because it invites us to ask, "What two opposing truths can I acknowledge that I embody?"

Continuing through the Aces, the Ace of Wands encourages curiosity and creativity in working with these contradictions. It helps to spark our curiosity by giving us energy to explore our shadows rather than suppress them, especially through journaling, art, or psychodrama where the shadow can become the lead character in a safe, contained space. This allows us to understand the shadow's purpose, reducing reactivity and fostering internal balance.

The Ace of Pentacles symbolizes the grounded, intentional work of assimilating our shadows with patience and self-compassion. This process is both vulnerable and experimental. For example, you may be irritated with a coworker and tempted to gossip. The Ace of Pentacles urges a purposeful pause: What are you really seeking? Before shadow work, you might have acted on this impulse. In the integration phase, you pause, identify your shadow and your need (perhaps for validation) and choose to express frustration constructively.

Finally, the Ace of Cups represents the healing and emotional fulfillment that follows integration. Its overflow doesn't reflect excess, but authentic growth. This overflow is evidence of our increasing capacity to love and accept all parts of ourselves and have patience and compassion for others. Like the overflowing cup, we are meant to expand beyond old limitations, nurturing the ever-evolving complexity of our humanness.

SHADOW INTEGRATION IN ACTION

I was working with a client who was experiencing significant difficulties in their relationship with their father. They frequently referred to him as a "gigantic narcissist" and expressed that he was solely concerned with his own needs. Week after week, they would enter my office, visibly frustrated, sit down with an exasperated sigh, and exclaim, "Wait until you hear what he did *this* week." They repeatedly identified behaviors such as interruption, lack of social awareness, inability to empathize, and an apparent disinterest in their life as central sources of their frustration. According to the client, their father only seemed interested in engaging with them when the conversation revolved around him.

Over several weeks, we processed their emotions and intense reactivity toward their father. Then in one session I decided to take a different approach and I asked them to consider instances where they might have exhibited similar behaviors as their father. Initially, they scoffed at the suggestion, and I feared it might have caused a rupture in our therapeutic relationship. However, after a prolonged silence, they quietly uttered two words: "Middle school." Their arms were crossed, and it was clear they were uncomfortable.

Sensing the importance of the moment, I gently encouraged them to elaborate. The client then recounted painful memories from their childhood when they were bullied and ostracized for behaviors such as interrupting their peers, habitually responding with "me too," and neglecting to show genuine interest in others—instead expecting their peers to listen to their exuberance over their latest hobby. The client said they felt like they had to hide their interests and that talking about themself was "bad."

Eventually, we began exploring how these early experiences might have contributed to the development of a shadow, which was now being triggered by their father, resulting in their own projection. The client's reactivity to their father's behavior was the client's way of putting more distance and space between themself and the behaviors they felt ashamed of as a child and now as an adult.

Over time, the client gained greater insight into themself, their neurodiversities, and the aspects of their personality that they had repressed because of those painful middle school experiences. This newfound awareness allowed them to develop a degree of empathy for their father. Their frustration regarding his lack of social skills and awareness decreased, and they became less reactive. This shift had a cascading effect, leading to a noticeable reduction in their overall anxiety and tension related to their father. While they continued to feel dissatisfied with the lack of reciprocal communication in their relationship, we were able to address additional ways to cope with this in subsequent sessions. The key takeaway is that by recognizing and integrating this shadow, the client achieved a deeper sense of self-awareness and contentment. They no longer felt controlled by the actions (or lack thereof) of their father.

EXERCISE: SHADOW INTEGRATION WITH THE ACES

This exercise helps you explore and integrate different aspects of your shadow using the four Aces of tarot. Each Ace corresponds to an aspect of shadow integration.

To begin, you will need your tarot deck and a journal for reflections. Start by pulling out the four Aces from your deck—Ace of Swords, Ace of Wands, Ace of Cups, and Ace of Pentacles. Lay them out in front of you, each representing a different integration aspect: assertiveness and clarity with the Ace of Swords, creativity and inspiration with the Ace of Wands, vulnerability and healing with the Ace of Cups, and practical application with the Ace of Pentacles. These cards will serve as a foundation for your exploration.

Next, shuffle the remaining cards in your deck and draw one card to accompany each Ace. These additional cards will offer deeper insights and practical guidance on how you can engage with and better understand the shadows you have explored on your shadow work journey. Use the card you pull to accompany each Ace as a guide to help you reflect on the questions below.

Ace of Swords

- What truth about yourself is this card trying to show you?

- Where have you been in denial, or afraid to speak your truth?

- What belief or inner conflict needs clarity?

Ace of Wands

- What passion, desire, or emotion are you repressing?

- How might this energy be trying to express itself?

- How can you give it voice through action or creativity?

Ace of Cups

- What feelings have you avoided or judged?

- What part of you feels unloved or unseen?

- How can you offer yourself more compassion?

Ace of Pentacles

- What practical step can you take to honor what you've discovered?

- How can you embody this awareness in your choices, boundaries, or habits?

- What needs to shift in your daily life now?

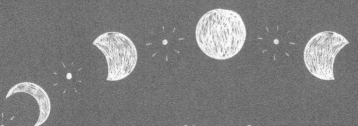

Chapter 8

Essential Exercises for Shadow Work

❦

Humans have a tendency to look for things in the places where it is easiest to search for them rather than in the places where the truth is more likely to be found.

- ESTHER PEREL

YOUR COMPREHENSIVE GUIDE

This chapter provides a comprehensive guide to working with the shadow through various exercises specifically designed to complement each stage of your shadow work journey as it has been outlined in this book. The exercises are organized by the chapters they complement, making it simple to return to them as you progress through the material. In addition to the exercises introduced throughout this book, this section includes new practices to further enhance your exploration.

These exercises are not meant to follow a strict order; rather, they are designed for you to craft your own shadow work journey. Take the time to browse the exercises, selecting one or two that resonate with where you are in your process. This section can be revisited repeatedly to offer clarity and direction as you continue your path toward shadow integration.

This is where you'll be putting your personal shadow journal to work, as you visit these practices and prompts again and again, each time making new discoveries and growing further on your path to wholeness and assimilation.

EMBRACING THE SHADOW

Welcome to Embracing the Shadow, a six-week journey designed to help you explore the hidden aspects of yourself through daily reflective prompts. Whether you choose to pull tarot cards or simply reflect and journal on each question, this practice invites you to peel back the layers of your inner world and confront the parts of yourself that have been tucked away in the shadows.

Over the next six weeks (30 days total, but time given for rest), you will navigate vulnerability, defense mechanisms, self-judgment, and more. Through this process, you will not only uncover the parts of yourself that have been ignored, but also practice integrating them to feel more whole and authentic. By the end of this journey, you will have a clearer under-standing of your shadow and the tools to continue your growth. This 30-day journey of reflective prompts can help to set the foundation for your shadow work experience.

Week 1: Vulnerability, Shame, and Defense Mechanisms

Day 1: What do I gain when I allow myself to be vulnerable?
Reflect on how vulnerability shapes your self-perception and relationships.

Day 2: When am I most reactive? What is this reactive part afraid of?
Explore what hidden fears trigger your defensiveness.

Day 3: What shame am I holding on to? How can I begin to release it?
Examine the roots of your shame and small, tangible steps to release its hold.

Day 4: What do I feel like I'm defending myself against?
How can I assess whether this defensiveness is serving me or limiting me?

Day 5: How can I nourish my inner artist?
Reflect on creative energy as a source of healing and expression.

Week 2: Patterns of Behavior and Self-Expression

Day 6: When does my practicality hold me back?
Challenge where overreliance on practicality stifles spontaneity or risk-taking.

Day 7: When do I stray from my long-term goals?
Explore how self-sabotage or fear may be misguiding you.

Day 8: What thoughts or ideas am I avoiding?
Consider how you can cultivate curiosity.

Day 9: How can I accept defeat without falling into self-deprecation?
Reflect on the difference between constructive self-reflection and harsh self-criticism.

Day 10: How can I express gratitude for the areas of my life where I am most fulfilled?
Explore what it would look like to shift your focus.

Week 3: Connection, Honesty, and Support

Day 11: What area of my life would I like to build upon?
What small actions can I take to begin this process?

Day 12: Who in my life have I not been paying attention to?
What value might they bring if I truly listen?

Day 13: When am I being dishonest with myself or others?
Explore moments of dishonesty and what they're protecting.

Day 14: How can I tell when I am adequately regulating my emotions?
What signs point to emotional dysregulation?

Day 15: Who can I rely on for support?
What prevents me from fully receiving that support?

Week 4: Transformation, Rigid Beliefs, and Shadow Work

Day 16: How does my rigidity limit my ability to grow, learn, or experience life?
Examine where inflexibility might be blocking opportunities for personal growth.

Day 17: What transformations am I welcoming into my life, and what am I resisting?
Explore your relationship to change and what it means for your shadow.

Day 18: How can I open myself up to more authentic connection?
Where can I seek out opportunities for deeper relationships?

Day 19: What adventures am I yearning for?
What do my daydreams reveal about unacknowledged desires or longings?

Day 20: What am I not paying attention to in my life right now?
What might be hiding in plain sight?

Week 5: Success, Acknowledgment, and Shadow Integration

Day 21: What is my relationship to success?
How might hidden fears or beliefs around success hold me back?

Day 22: What am I refusing to acknowledge about myself or my life?
How does this refusal impact me?

Day 23: What personal or universal mysteries fascinate me?
What do these curiosities reveal about my values?

Day 24: What judgments do I make about others that reflect things I dislike in myself?
Reflect on how projecting your inner struggles onto others might reveal hidden aspects of your shadow.

Day 25: What do I seek to control in my life?
  How can I work toward surrendering control in a healthy way?

Week 6: Grief, Rituals, and Desire

Day 26: How can I create time and space to process my grief or disappointment?
  Acknowledge where unprocessed grief or loss may be residing in your shadow.

Day 27: When do I feel truly satisfied?
  Reflect on moments of satisfaction and how they align with your values and desires.

Day 28: In what ways can I invite ritual into my life?
  How can ritual support my shadow work journey?

Day 29: How can I be more in tune with my deepest desires?
  Explore how you can tap into and honor your own wants and needs.

Day 30: Reflect on the past six weeks. What has this journey revealed about your shadow?
  What steps can you take moving forward to continue integrating and embracing it?

SEEKING STABILITY

This spread is designed to help you identify and manage emotional turbulence as you embark on your shadow work journey. By using the cards to explore the emotional landscape you are entering, you can gain valuable insight into what emotions may arise, how to regulate these feelings, and how to create a nurturing environment during this process. This exercise invites you to reflect on your emotional readiness and prepare yourself with practical tools for self-care and regulation during shadow work.

Card 1: Turbulence

- What difficult emotions should you be mindful of as you embark on a shadow work journey?

- How do these emotions make you feel physically and mentally?

Card 2: Regulation

- What strategies can you use to regulate yourself when you feel overwhelmed by shadow work?

Card 3: Safety

- How can you create a supportive, calming space for your shadow work journey?

COMPLEXES AND PROJECTIONS

Card 1: A Shadow

This card represents a shadow aspect of yourself—an unresolved part of your psyche that may be hidden or repressed. Reflect on what this card reveals about the part of you that is being neglected, disowned, or rejected.

Card 2: Its Complex

This card represents the deeper psychological complex tied to the shadow. What belief, thought, story, or emotional pattern is driving this shadow? This could relate to past experiences, traumas, or learned behaviors.

Card 3: How It Projects

This card reveals how your shadow manifests or projects onto others or situations in your life. How does this shadow affect your relationships, decision-making, or emotional responses?

Card 4: What to Do About It

This card offers guidance on how to manage, integrate, or work through this shadow. What steps can you take to face this shadow and transform its influence? How can you bring awareness and compassion to this part of yourself?

THE DORMANT GOLDEN SHADOW

The shadow also contains golden qualities: the dormant, often overlooked gifts and potential that we have yet to fully embrace. By exploring these parts, we not only enhance our sense of Self but also allow for the emergence of untapped creativity and confidence. By examining the dormant energy within us and reflecting on how our lives might change if we embraced this potential, we take an important step in shadow integration. The following prompts encourage us to identify what holds us back and consider how awakening this energy could transform our lives moving forward.

Card 1: Dormant golden shadow energy to be awakened

Card 2: What would I be doing differently if I embraced this energy?

Card 3: What currently stands in my way of embracing this energy?

Card 4: What role might this awakened energy play in my life moving forward?

YOU AS THE GOLDEN SHADOW

This exercise aims to facilitate this process of exploring the golden shadow and serves as a complement to traditional shadow work. Embracing the golden shadow allows us to step into our fullest potential, and become a more aligned, authentic, and balanced version of ourselves.

Card 1: You as your golden shadow

Card 2: The obstacle(s) that block you from embracing a golden shadow

Cards 3–5: Steps to take to help you navigate the obstacles

SHADOW AS ABOVE, SHADOW SO BELOW

This four-card spread offers insight into the forces that contribute to the strengthening of shadow material. To begin, you may either shuffle the deck and intuitively draw a card to represent your shadow or select a card that has previously been identified as a shadow based on earlier exercises within this book. This card will serve as the central focus of the spread, placed in the middle of your layout.

Next, shuffle the deck once more and draw two additional cards. The card placed below the shadow card signifies the past influences that contributed to the formation of this shadow. This card helps reveal the historical or foundational experiences that gave rise to this particular shadow material. The card placed above the shadow card represents current influences that are perpetuating or reinforcing the shadow in your present life.

Finally, draw a fourth card and place it horizontally across the shadow card. This card symbolizes a potential pathway for acknowledging and integrating the shadow, allowing it to have less control over your daily life. It provides a bridge between recognition and transformation, guiding you toward a more conscious and balanced relationship with your shadow self.

See the layout on page 163.

REFLECT

- What emotions surfaced during this exercise, and how do they inform your understanding of the shadow's role in your behavior or relationships?

- How does recognizing the influences of the past and present empower you to take responsibility for how this shadow shows up in your life today?

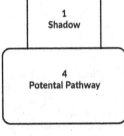

SHADOWS IN RELATIONSHIPS

This exercise helps you explore how you might project your shadow onto others and how this can affect your relationships. Start by reflecting on someone in your life who triggers a strong emotional response, whether it's irritation, jealousy, or resentment. Pay attention to the specific traits or behaviors in this person that evoke these feelings in you and write down what you dislike or judge about them.

Next, consider how these traits might reflect aspects of your own shadow—parts of yourself that you haven't fully integrated or acknowledged. It might be helpful to pull a tarot card to represent your shadow in this context and use it as a guide for deeper reflection.

REFLECT

- How does this trait reflect a part of you that you find uncomfortable?

- What insights can you gain from recognizing this dynamic?

Shadow Boundaries

This exercise helps you explore how difficulties with setting healthy boundaries may be connected to your shadow and how this impacts your relationships. Begin by reflecting on a relationship in which you frequently feel drained, overextended, or frustrated. Identify the specific boundary violations occurring in this dynamic, such as being overly available or engaging in people-pleasing behaviors. Consider how your shadow may be driving these actions; maybe it's a fear of rejection or a strong desire for approval. You may want to pull a tarot card to symbolize the shadow influencing your boundary struggles, offering further insight into this issue. Reflect on the following questions, or pull a tarot card to offer additional insight.

REFLECT

- What boundary is being crossed in this relationship?

- What shadow aspect is preventing you from setting a healthy boundary?

- How can you communicate and enforce this boundary moving forward?

RITUAL FOR BALANCING LOGIC AND MAGICK

This exercise for balancing logic and magick invites you to explore the dynamic tension between these two aspects of yourself through a personalized ritual.

Begin by setting up a ritual space that reflects both your logical and magickal sides. Include items that symbolize clarity and reason, such as a plant or leaf for logic, alongside elements representing intuition and mystery, like a crystal for magick. As you arrange your space, reflect on how these objects embody the balance between rationality and mysticism within you.

Next, pull two tarot cards—one to represent your logical side and one to symbolize your magickal side. Take a moment to observe how these cards interact, reflecting on the insights they offer about the relationship between logic and magick in your life.

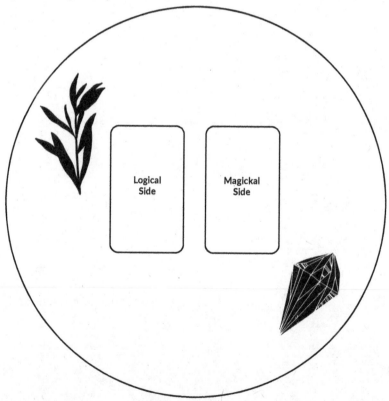

With your ritual space and cards in front of you, reflect on roles that both logic and magick will play in your personal growth and shadow work journey. Consider how these forces coexist within you and how they can work together to deepen your understanding of yourself.

REFLECT

- What qualities do you associate with the objects you've chosen to represent logic and magick in your ritual space, and how do these qualities manifest in your daily life?

- In what ways have logic and magick supported or challenged your personal growth?

- What resistance or tension arises when you think about merging logic and magick, and how might you begin to release or work through this?

EXPLORING THE ARCHETYPAL SHADOW THROUGH DEATH

This exercise, centered around the Death card, is a powerful way to prepare yourself for a shadow work journey. By working through the prompts, you are invited to consider the parts of yourself that are ready for change and transformation. The process of acknowledging what needs to be released, what parts of you will experience grief in that process, and how you might accept what comes next is an essential step in shadow work. This reflective exercise allows for a deeper understanding of your inner world, offering a framework to confront and integrate your shadow aspects as you navigate a shadow work journey.

Anchor: The Death card

Card 1: What part of my shadow is ready for integration?

Card 2: What might this integration look like?

Card 3: How will this integration transform my life?

Card 4: What parts of me will grieve when this change occurs?

Card 5: What do I have to look forward to by welcoming this integration and transformation?

FINDING YOUR SHADOW SUIT

In the same way shadow material can be identified in how we judge others, it can also be identified in how we judge the cards. For example, cards that elicit strong emotional reactions might have shadow material hidden within them. The same can be said for every suit of the tarot, each of which carries distinct energies that may align with or challenge different aspects of our unconscious selves.

Consider the suit in the tarot that resonates with you the most. Reflect on what it is about this suit that feels aligned with your personality, values, or worldview. What draws you to this particular suit, and how does it align with your self-perception?

Conversely, think about the suit that evokes discomfort or unease within you. How might your own behaviors, attitudes, or thought patterns correspond with the qualities of this suit? In what ways could you be distancing yourself from the energy of this suit due to its activation of potential shadow material?

Identify Your Favorite Suit

As you reflect on the suits, identify the one that you are most drawn to—the suit that feels most aligned with your personality, worldview, or emotional state. Ask yourself the following questions and journal your responses:

- What qualities of this suit resonate most deeply with you?

- How does this suit reflect your strengths, values, and personal philosophy?

- In what ways does this suit align with the aspects of yourself that you feel comfortable expressing to the world?

Explore Your Discomfort

Next, focus on the suit that makes you feel uneasy or uncomfortable—the one that you tend to feel annoyed with when it appears in your readings. As you explore this discomfort, use the following reflective questions to guide your journaling:

- What specific feelings arise when you think about this suit? Fear, irritation, or avoidance?

- How might these feelings reveal unacknowledged or repressed parts of yourself?

- In what ways could this suit be reflecting shadow material, such as hidden fears, insecurities, or unresolved conflicts?

Engage in a Dialogue with the Suits

Select one card from each of the two suits you've identified (the suit you resonate with and the suit that evokes discomfort). Place them in front of you and engage in a reflective dialogue with the cards. Consider the following:

- What does the card from your favorite suit have to teach you about your strengths and how you show up in the world?

- What does the card from the uncomfortable suit reveal about your shadow and areas of potential growth?

- What might these two cards say to each other?

CONVERSING WITH THE CARDS

In this exercise, we will confront and engage with the cards that evoke strong reactions or discomfort within us. By observing and conversing with these cards, we can work to better understand our initial responses and potentially discover a shadow.

Pull or intentionally choose a card to represent yourself; this will be Card A. Select a card that you have difficulty with or have a strong reaction to; this will be Card B. You may also choose to continue using the cards from the previous exercise in this one.

Place Card A and Card B next to each other. Observe and reflect on each card.

- What do you notice about each card?

- What similarities and differences exist between the cards?

- What might create a link or bond between them?

- What might create distance or space between them?

Now practice conversing with the cards. Use the formula below as a general guideline to begin the conversation. This exercise is inspired by the Gestalt Empty Chair technique. You will be speaking on behalf of each card, as if you had embodied the archetype.

Card A begins by expressing feelings about Card B:

Card A: "I feel _____ about [Card B] because _____, and I struggle with _____."

Card B responds with curiosity: "I wonder if that's because _____?"

Card A answers: "I think I feel that way because of _____."

REFLECT

- What did you discover about the conversation between the card that elicits a strong reaction within you and the card you chose to represent yourself?

EXERCISE: AVOIDANCE AND ACCEPTANCE

Reflecting on a card you have a strong reaction to, shuffle your deck and pull two additional cards.

Card 1 represents something you *want* to hear from this card.

Card 2 represents something you *don't want* to hear from this card.

THE SHADOW SPIRAL

This exercise is designed to help you step into your shadow world, using the archetype of the Moon card as a central guide. The Moon represents the hidden, unconscious aspects of the Self, making it a perfect companion for shadow work. This exercise encourages you to create a spiral around the Moon card to explore various layers of your shadow, from the most hidden aspects to those that are more in your conscious awareness.

Begin by shuffling your tarot deck while meditating on the Moon card as the anchor for this journey into your unconscious. Place the Moon card in the center of your workspace. See the diagram on page 174.

Next, create the spiral by pulling three cards for the first layer. These cards will reflect the aspects of yourself that you have deeply repressed or denied. Place them in a tight semicircle around the Moon. Reflect on these cards and journal about the hidden emotions, fears, or traits that they might reveal.

For the second layer, pull another three cards (cards 4–6). These represent parts of your shadow that are beginning to emerge into your conscious awareness, perhaps showing up as certain behavior or thought patterns, or emotional triggers. Place these cards in a wider semicircle around the first layer and reflect on how these shadow aspects are beginning to influence your life. Journal about how they may manifest in your thoughts, actions, or relationships.

The third and outermost layer represents the shadow aspects that are already in your conscious awareness but have not been fully integrated. Pull three more cards (cards 7–9) to symbolize these shadow traits and place them in the outer circle. Reflect on how these traits impact your decisions, relationships, and self-perception, and journal about how you can begin working toward integrating these aspects.

After completing the spiral, pull a final card to represent a pathway toward integration. Place this card on top of the Moon and reflect on how it can guide you in acknowledging, accepting, and integrating the shadow aspects revealed during the exercise.

By engaging in this process, you allow yourself to explore and embrace the many layers of your shadow, moving toward greater self-awareness and personal growth. Journaling throughout the exercise helps deepen the insights you gain from the cards and supports the ongoing journey of shadow integration.

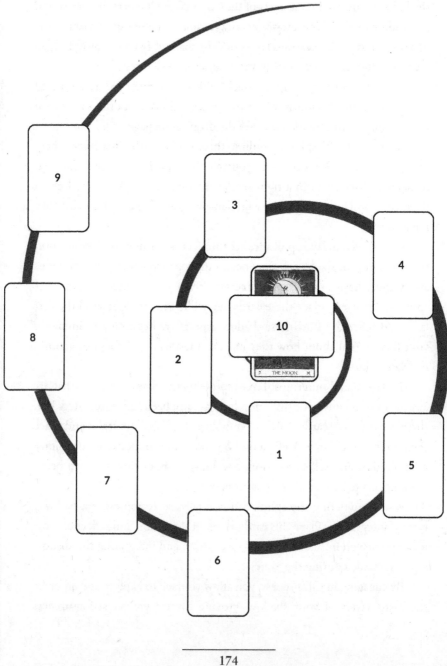

ANCESTRAL SHADOW MAP

The purpose of this exercise is to help you identify specific emotional or behavioral patterns that have been passed down through generations.

Begin by drawing a family tree or "shadow map" with yourself at the top, and at least three generations (parents, grandparents, and great-grandparents). For each generation, write down any known emotional patterns, fears, or behaviors that you are aware of, such as emotional avoidance, hyper-independence, or anger. You may choose to assign a tarot card to each person and then pull a card to represent possible emotional and behavioral patterns or shadows linked to them.

As you reflect on these patterns, consider how they may have been passed down to you. Even if you are unsure of the emotional lives of your ancestors, use your imagination and hypothesize what their behaviors might have been, considering the environment or circumstances they faced.

Finish the exercise by journaling about the shadows you feel most connected to. Reflect on how these generational patterns affect your own life today, bringing awareness to the ways in which you may continue to carry or act upon these inherited shadows.

> **Note:** If you don't have access to your ancestral history (whether through adoption, separation, or circumstances beyond your control), you are invited to think about folks who have had impacts on your overall upbringing—peers, teachers, etc. The aim here isn't genealogical accuracy, it's emotional insight and self-compassion. However, feel free to modify or skip this exercise if it does not resonate with you.

REFLECT

- What patterns or behaviors do you notice recurring across generations?

  How have these patterns shaped your family's interactions, values, or ways of dealing with emotions?

- How do you see these generational shadows showing up in your own life?

  In what ways have you consciously or unconsciously adopted these behaviors or emotional responses?

- What type of environment or circumstances may have contributed to your ancestors developing these patterns?

  How might societal, cultural, or historical factors have influenced their behaviors, and how does that perspective help you understand these shadows today?

- What strengths or positive traits might have emerged as a result of these challenges?

  Are there any lessons or sources of resilience that you've inherited alongside these shadows?

- In what areas of your life do you feel particularly connected to your family's emotional patterns or behaviors?

  How do these inherited traits affect your relationships, work, or personal growth?

CIRCLE OF THE QUEENS

This exercise invites you to engage in shadow integration with the wisdom and support of the four Queens in tarot. Each Queen embodies distinct archetypal qualities that can guide you through the complex layers of your shadow, offering unique perspectives on how to approach self-exploration and healing. Acting as a circle of counselors, the Queen of Wands, Queen of Cups, Queen of Swords, and Queen of Pentacles all offer insight into different dimensions of your shadow and provide wisdom for exploring and integrating these parts.

Begin by shuffling and pulling a card to represent the specific shadow aspect you wish to explore. Or if you have a particular shadow archetype you have been working with, use that card. This card will act as the anchor card of your exercise, placed in the center of your space. Once you've identified your shadow, you will cast a circle with the Queens by laying each Queen around your shadow card. See the diagram on page 178.

Start by working with the Queen of Wands, who brings courage and empowerment. Reflect on the following:

- When you think about the more challenging parts of yourself, what might help you feel more empowered to face them?

- What small, courageous steps can you take to start accepting aspects of yourself that you've been avoiding?

Then move on to the Queen of Cups to explore the emotional depths of your shadow.

- How might you begin to connect more deeply with your emotions, particularly those you tend to shy away from?

- As you reflect on unhealed emotions, what comes up for you?

- How can you start to hold space for these feelings?

Next, spend time with the Queen of Swords, who will help you gain clarity and approach your shadow with intellectual honesty.

- What truths about yourself have you been reluctant to acknowledge, and how might that reluctance be influencing your current situation?

- How do you think your view of yourself might shift if you allow yourself to look at your shadow with a more objective, clear perspective?

Finally, work with the Queen of Pentacles to ground this exploration in practical action.

- What realistic and sustainable changes can you make in your daily life that will help you process and integrate your shadow work?

- How do you plan to incorporate self-compassion and care as you continue this journey of self-exploration and healing?

Take time to journal about the insights each Queen has offered. Reflect on the guidance they have provided and how their strengths can support your journey toward balance and wholeness. To make this exercise more robust, you could pull an accompanying card for each Queen to act as their voice when reflecting on the questions above.

INTEGRATION ASSESSMENT

The Integration Assessment spread is designed to assess your progress in shadow work by identifying which aspects of your shadow have been acknowledged, partially integrated, or remain undiscovered. By pulling two cards for each phase—*Integrated*, *In Progress*, and *Undiscovered*—you will gain insight into the areas of your shadow that have been embraced and those that still require attention.

Begin by pulling two cards for each of the following positions:

- **Integrated:** These cards represent aspects of your shadow that you have already acknowledged and integrated into your conscious self. Reflect on how these aspects have influenced your self-awareness, personal growth, and daily life.

- **In Progress:** The cards in this position show parts of your shadow that you are actively working on but have yet to fully integrate. These shadow elements may need further attention and exploration as you continue on your journey.

- **Undiscovered:** These cards symbolize the shadow aspects that remain unacknowledged or untouched. They represent the areas of your psyche that may hold potential for future growth and transformation.

After pulling your cards, use the following questions to guide your reflection:

- Which aspects of your shadow have you already acknowledged and begun to integrate? How has this awareness influenced the way you navigate your inner world and your daily life?

- What parts of your shadow have you become aware of but have yet to fully embrace or integrate into your conscious Self? How might these areas need more attention as you continue your shadow work journey?

- Which shadow aspect are you still working to integrate? Select one card from your spread that resonates with this ongoing process. Keep this card visible or accessible as an anchor for future reflection and use it as a reminder of the work still to be done.

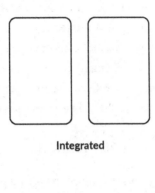

Integrated

In Progress

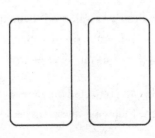

Undiscovered

SHADOW INSIGHT AND
INTEGRATION AWARENESS

The Shadow Insight and Integration spread is designed to provide a comprehensive view of your shadow work journey, helping you to reflect on the progress you have made and the deeper energies you have encountered along the way. This spread invites you to look back at where you started, examine where you are now, and explore the shadows you have encountered as well as the dormant energies you have awakened. This spread is an opportunity to reflect on the transformative process of shadow work and how it has shaped your relationship with yourself and the world around you.

Begin by pulling cards for each position in the spread:

- **Where I was:** Representing your starting point in shadow work, the challenges or experiences that initiated your journey.

- **Where I am:** Revealing your current state, highlighting the growth, awareness, and ongoing processes within your shadow work.

- **Shadows I've encountered:** Showing the shadows that you've discovered during your journey and how they have impacted you.

- **Dormant energies I've awakened:** Bringing forward the hidden strengths, potential, or untapped resources that have been awakened through your shadow work.

Once you have pulled and reflected on your cards, deepen your understanding by answering the following questions:

- What is the difference between where you were when your shadow work journey began and where you are now?

- How have the shadows you encountered influenced the way you experience yourself and the world around you today?

- In what ways have you embraced or welcomed the dormant energies that you have awakened? How do they regularly show up in your life currently?

TAROT SHADOWS

Each card in the tarot can be categorized based on a shadow it could be associated with. To aid you in working with the shadow and tarot together, use this list of shadow qualities as a quick reference, or mode of inspiration, when stepping into shadow work. You're also encouraged to create your own list of shadows. We all have a unique personal relationship to tarot, so your own associations with the cards may differ from what is presented here, and that's okay!

RECKLESS / IMPULSIVE / IMPATIENT

- The Fool
- Knight of Wands
- The Chariot
- Ace of Wands

MANIPULATIVE / ALOOF / INSENSITIVE

- The Magician
- The Moon
- King of Cups
- Knight of Cups
- The Hierophant
- Two of Cups

SELF-INDULGENT / UNAPPROACHABLE / SUPERFICIAL

- The Hermit
- Four of Swords
- High Priestess
- Nine of Wands
- Seven of Cups
- Eight of Wands

ARROGANT / VAIN / CONTROLLING

- The Emperor
- Six of Wands
- The Sun

- King of Wands
- Queen of Wands

FEARFUL / HELPLESS / SELF-DOUBT

- Strength
- Nine of Swords
- Death
- Two of Swords
- Two of Wands
- Five of Pentacles
- Eight of Cups

ADDICTION / MATERIALISM / GREED

- The Devil
- Ace of Pentacles
- King of Pentacles
- Nine of Cups
- Four of Pentacles
- Six of Pentacles

MARTYRDOM / INDECISIVE / PROCRASTINATION

- The Hanged One
- Seven of Pentacles
- Knight of Pentacles
- Queen of Cups
- Two of Pentacles
- Three of Wands
- Ten of Wands

OVERLY COMPETITIVE / DISHONEST / PARANOID

- Five of Wands
- Five of Swords
- Seven of Wands
- Page of Wands
- The Tower

HOPELESS / DESPONDENT / DISILLUSIONED

- The Star
- Ten of Cups
- Five of Cups
- Page of Cups
- Ace of Cups
- Eight of Swords

COMPLACENT / UNRELIABLE / AVOIDANT

- Four of Wands
- The World
- Nine of Pentacles
- Three of Pentacles
- Ten of Pentacles
- Eight of Pentacles
- Six of Swords

BETRAYAL / VENGEFUL / HARSH

- Three of Swords
- Seven of Swords
- Ten of Swords
- Knight of Swords
- Wheel of Fortune

GOSSIP / NEGLECTFUL / HYPOCRITICAL

- The Empress
- Three of Cups
- Temperance
- Queen of Pentacles
- Page of Pentacles
- The Lovers
- Page of Swords

CRITICAL / JUDGMENTAL / CALLOUS

- Justice
- Queen of Swords
- King of Swords
- Judgement
- Ace of Swords
- Four of Cups
- Six of Cups

A FINAL NOTE

As you close this book, remember that the journey of shadow work is one of courage, curiosity, and continuous growth. Discovering and integrating our shadows is not about perfection, or even crossing a finish line; it's about giving ourselves permission to be complex and layered. This journey is about finding compassion for the parts of us we want to keep hidden and, in turn, having patience and compassion for others. The insights, archetypes, and reflections you have encountered here are just the beginning of a life-long exploration. My hope is that this book serves as a trusted companion on your path toward self-compassion, authenticity, and shadow integration for years to come.

ACKNOWLEDGMENTS

My creative journey has been enriched and uplifted by an incredible network of support, encouragement, and love. To Ashlee, my platonic soulmate and unwavering pillar of support, thank you for always being by my side. Rob, your friendship and keen eye have been invaluable to my work—I'm grateful for every insight and inspiration you've shared with me. To Sydney and Shailey, may this work inspire you as I strive every day to be a role model worthy of your admiration.

To Anthony, your support has turned my creative dreams into realities, and I am endlessly grateful for you. My heartfelt thanks to my parents, who have always encouraged my independence, allowing me the freedom to explore and create my own life path. Jane and Norm, your support, love, and friendship are deeply cherished. To Andrew, Daylina, and Heather—your unwavering encouragement, support, and belief in me have meant the world.

To anyone who has supported *The Tarot Diagnosis*, or been a member of its community, The Symposium, thank you for finding value in this work and giving me a platform to explore, learn, and grow alongside you. Please know that your support and kindness have been felt deeply and are appreciated beyond measure. Thank you for being a part of this journey with me.

To my therapy clients, thank you for trusting me with your stories and for showing me what resilience, vulnerability, and growth truly look like. I am honored to be your therapist.

THE TAROT DIAGNOSIS PODCAST

The Tarot Diagnosis is a podcast that invites you to explore the mysteries of tarot through psychological, philosophical, and humanistic lenses. Join Shannon Knight, a Johns Hopkins trained psychotherapist and tarot enthusiast, as she offers insightful, therapeutic perspectives on tarot and the human experience.

Blending her knowledge of the cards with a touch of intuition, Shannon seeks to unlock new ways of understanding ourselves and those around us. Each episode, she dives deep into the meanings of the tarot, offering listeners an opportunity to explore how these archetypes connect to their own cognitive and emotional experiences.

Some episodes take listeners on solo expeditions into philosophical and psychological landscapes, while others feel like intimate discussions among friends, colleagues, and deep thinkers who share riveting and meaningful perspectives on life and tarot.

You can learn more about *The Tarot Diagnosis* podcast by visiting *TheTarotDiagnosis.com*, following the podcast on Instagram @TheTarot Diagnosis, or by listening to the podcast wherever you find music, audiobooks, or podcasts.

REFERENCES

Baker, P. (2014). *Austin Osman Spare: The Occult Life of London's Legendary Artist*. North Atlantic Books.

Beck, J. S. (2011). *Cognitive Behavior Therapy: Basics and Beyond* (2nd ed.). Guilford Press.

Bly, R. (1988). *A Little Book on the Human Shadow*. Harper & Row.

British Psychodrama Association. (2021). *Brief History of Psychodrama. psychodrama.org.uk*

Brown, B. (2006). Shame resilience theory: A grounded theory study on women and shame. *Families in Society: The Journal of Contemporary Social Services. doi.org/10.1606/1044-3894.3483*

Conway, D. J. (2001). *A Little Book of Altar Magic*. Crossing Press.

Dore, J. (2021). *Tarot for Change: Using the Cards for Self-Care, Acceptance, and Growth*. Penguin Life.

Erikson, E. H. (1959). *Identity and the Life Cycle: Selected Papers*. International Universities Press.

Freud, S. (1990). *The Ego and the Id* (J. Strachey, Ed.; P. Gay, Introduction). W. W. Norton & Company. (Original work published 1923.)

Gamache, C. M. (2012). An opposing self. *doi.org/10.28971/142012GC32*

Greer, M. K. (2019). *Tarot for Your Self: A Workbook for the Inward Journey* (35th anniversary ed.). Weiser Books.

Helbert, K. (2011). *Creating Shrines and Altars for Healing from Grief.* GoodTherapy. *goodtherapy.org*

Hobson, N. M., Schroeder, J., & Risen, J. L. (2018). The psychology of rituals: An integrative review and process-based framework. *Personality and Social Psychology Review, 22*(3), 260–284.

Hopper, S. I., Murray, S. L., Ferrara, L. R., & Singleton, J. K. (2019). Effectiveness of diaphragmatic breathing for reducing physiological and psychological stress in adults: A quantitative systematic review. *JBI Database of Systematic Reviews and Implementation Reports, 17*(9), 1855–1876. *doi.org/10.11124/JBISRIR-2017-003848*

Horney, K. (1950). *Neurosis and Human Growth: The Struggle Toward Self-Realization*. W. W. Norton & Company.

Hughes, A. (2025). *Mystic Storyteller: A Writer's Guide to Using the Tarot for Creative Inspiration*. La Panthère Studio.

Johnson, R. A. (1991). *Owning Your Own Shadow: Understanding the Dark Side of the Psyche*. HarperOne.

Jung, C. G. (1916/1953). *The Psychology of the Unconscious* (B. M. Hinkle, Trans.). Moffat, Yard & Company.

Jung, C. G. (1951). *Aion: Researches into the Phenomenology of the Self*. Princeton University Press.

Jung, C. G. (1953). *Psychology and Alchemy* (2nd ed.). Routledge & Kegan Paul.

Jung, C. G. (1953). *Psychological Reflections: An Anthology of the Writings of C.G. Jung, Volume 3* (J. Jacobi, Ed.). Princeton University Press.

Jung, C. G. (1959). *The Archetypes and the Collective Unconscious* (R. F. C. Hull, Trans.). Princeton University Press. (Original work published 1953.)

Jung, C. G. (1966). Psychological Aspects of the Personality. In H. Read, M. Fordham, & G. Adler (Eds.), The Collected Works of C. G. Jung (Vol. 7: Two essays on analytical psychology) (R. F. C. Hull, Trans., 2nd ed., pp. 305-333). Princeton University Press. (Original work published 1946.)

Jung, C. G. (1966). *The Practice of Psychotherapy: Essays on the Psychology of the Transference and Other Subjects*. Princeton University Press.

Jung, C. G. (2009). *The Red Book: Liber Novus: A Reader's Edition* (S. Shamdasani, Ed.). W. W. Norton & Company.

Kleingeld, A., van Mierlo, H., & Arends, L. (2011). The effect of goal setting on group performance: A meta-analysis. *Journal of Applied Psychology, 96*(6), 1289–1304.

Knight, S. (2024). Functions of the Shadow: Complexes and Projections (Episode 144) [Audio podcast episode]. In *The Tarot Diagnosis*. The Tarot Diagnosis LLC.

Knight, S. (2024). The Golden Shadow (Episode 137) [Audio podcast episode]. In *The Tarot Diagnosis*. The Tarot Diagnosis LLC.

Knight, S. (2024). Individuation and the World (Episode 130) [Audio podcast episode]. In *The Tarot Diagnosis*. The Tarot Diagnosis LLC.

Matthews, G. (2015). Goal research summary. Paper presented at the 9th Annual International Conference of the Psychology Research Unit of Athens Institute for Education and Research (ATINER), Athens, Greece.

McKay, M., Wood, J. C., & Brantley, J. (2019). *The Dialectical Behavior Therapy Skills Workbook: Practical DBT Exercises for Learning Mindfulness, Interpersonal Effectiveness, Emotion Regulation, and Distress Tolerance*. New Harbinger Publications.

Michigan Psychodrama Center. (n.d.). *Jacob Levy Moreno and Psychodrama. michiganpsychodramacenter.com*

Neumann, E. (1990). *Depth Psychology and a New Ethic*. Shambhala.

Neumann, E. (1990). *The Origins and History of Consciousness* (R. F. C. Hull, Trans.). Princeton University Press.

Pollack, R. (2019). *Seventy-Eight Degrees of Wisdom: A Tarot Journey to Self-Awareness* (New ed.). Weiser Books.

Porges, S. W., & Porges, S. (2023). *Our Polyvagal World: How Safety and Trauma Change Us*. W. W. Norton & Company.

Quinn, P. (2009). *Tarot for Life: Reading the Cards for Everyday Guidance and Growth*. Quest Books.

Rogers, C. R. (1951). *Client-Centered Therapy: Its Current Practice, Implications, and Theory*. Houghton Mifflin.

Schwartz, R. C. (2020). *IFS Therapy* (2nd ed.). Guilford Press.

Schwartz, R. (2023). *Introduction to Internal Family Systems*. Sounds True.

Siegel, D. J. (1999). *The Developing Mind: How Relationships and the Brain Interact to Shape Who We Are*. Guilford Press.

Stefan, B. (2016). The persona and the shadow in analytic psychology and existentialist philosophy. *Philobiblon. Transilvanian Journal of Multidisciplinary Research in Humanities, 21*(1), 84–94.

Tseng, A. A. (2022). Scientific evidence of health benefits by practicing mantra meditation: Narrative review. *International Journal of Yoga, 15*(2), 89–95.

University of Tampa. (n.d.). *History of the University of Tampa. ut.edu*

Vago, D. R., & Silbersweig, D. A. (2012). Self-awareness, self-regulation, and self-transcendence (S-ART): A framework for understanding the neurobiological mechanisms of mindfulness. *Frontiers in Human Neuroscience, 6,* 296.

Van Gennep, A. (1909). *Rite de Passage.* Émile Nourry.

Von Franz, M.-L. (1980). *Jung's Studies in Astrology and Alchemy.* Shambhala.

Wen, B. (2015). *Holistic Tarot: An Integrative Approach to Using Tarot for Personal Growth.* North Atlantic Books.

Yehuda, R., et al. (2005). Transgenerational effects of posttraumatic stress disorder in babies of mothers exposed to the World Trade Center attacks during pregnancy. *The Journal of Clinical Endocrinology & Metabolism, 90*(7), 4115–4118.

Yehuda, R., et al. (2016). Holocaust exposure induced intergenerational effects on FKBP5 methylation. *Biological Psychiatry, 80*(5), 372–380.

Zweig, C., & Abrams, J., et al. (Eds.). (1991). *Meeting the Shadow: The Hidden Power of the Dark Side of Human Nature.* TarcherPerigee.

ABOUT THE AUTHOR

Shannon Knight is a licensed psychotherapist with a master of science degree in Clinical Mental Health Counseling from Johns Hopkins University and a bachelor of arts degree in Applied Clinical Psychology from the Florida Institute of Technology.

Shannon is the host of *The Tarot Diagnosis* podcast, where she demystifies therapy and tarot by exploring the human experience through tarot archetypes. Each episode, she offers listeners the opportunity to connect tarot to their own cognitive, emotional, and life experiences. In addition to her podcast, Shannon has built a vibrant and inclusive community of tarot and psychology enthusiasts who are interested in understanding the deeper connections between mental health and tarot.

Drawing from years of experience in psychotherapy and her fascination with tarot, Shannon brings a compassionate, thoughtful, and evocative voice to the conversation around self-awareness and healing. Shannon's work is for those who are curious about blending traditional therapeutic practices with intuitive and creative tools, encouraging readers and listeners alike to explore their own shadows, develop self-compassion, and embrace the complexity of all of their parts.